NEST

A MEMOIR OF HOME ON THE MOVE

CATRIONA TURNER

WBP
Word Bothy Press

WORD BOTHY PRESS

A version of Chapter 33, 'The Gate', was first published in the anthology *Life on the Move*.

Paperback ISBN: 978-1-7393608-0-1

Ebook ISBN: 978-1-7393608-1-8

Cover design by Paul Palmer-Edwards

Published by Word Bothy Press

For Michael, who found home in me before I found it in myself

CONTENTS

PART ONE: RUE DU CHANOINE LABORDE, PAU

SHALL WE GO HOME NOW?

H e used the word 'home' with reckless abandon from the very beginning.
It was on our second date that Michael broke away from a kiss, stared
into my eyes and said, 'You feel like home to me.'

The intensity floored me, then swept me up. It was irresistible as much as it
was bewildering. My response was to hold his face and lean back in, knowing
that a new adventure was ahead, even if I couldn't understand quite what he
meant. Home for me had only ever been a place – maybe two places.

We had connected online, both just into our thirties. We bonded over books
and travel for a few days of emailing, before meeting for the first time. In the bar,
we exchanged stories of that summer's travel – his to China, mine to Australia –
more about books, and after the waiter in the Italian restaurant read the specials,
we said almost in unison, 'She lost me at mushrooms.'

The following year, on our first holiday together in Italy, we would be
strolling around Florence, or Venice, stopping here and there for gelato, or a Per-
oni, or taking in the glories of Renaissance frescoes or the Tuscan countryside,
and he would say, 'Shall we go home now?' I would stare back, brow furrowed.
'Are you not having a good time?' But then I would realise, oh, he means, *go
back to the hotel*. Calling a hotel room 'home' made no sense to me. But home,
to him, meant wherever we were together, even then.

Ours was the romance I'd been looking for, that I'd been impatient for all my
life, except that of course by the time we met I had settled into my independence.
When I moved in with him, it was a wrench to give up my flat, the home I
had created, that I'd bought with my own money, that I had furnished and
decorated; my nest that was exactly as I wanted it, no longer shared with family

or flatmates. That flat, in Aberdeen, the city I had chosen as home in my adulthood, had become part of my identity for years, along with the teaching career that meant I was a known face for hundreds of young Aberdonians, and my musical theatre hobby that saw me perform on stages in the city's granite buildings several times a year.

His flat, on the other hand, was a base, where he spent fifty percent of his time – the rest in a bunk on an oil platform in the middle of the North Sea, then later in a company apartment in Nigeria where he worked on rotation. I moved in and made it mine, one hundred percent of the time – except it was filled with his inherited furniture, and he had designed and planned his new kitchen before we met. It was only when we installed a new bathroom together that it really started to feel like a nest for me.

That was when his company came up with the offer: three years working at their office in southern France.

It was too good an opportunity to pass up, the adventure that had been in the air from the start. So I packed up again. My books and his books – barely even 'our' books yet – went back into boxes to be stored in the attic, along with the rest of the possessions deemed unnecessary for our temporary expatriation.

His job started in June. I stayed behind to finish up the teaching year and organise our shipment to Pau in south-west France, near the border with Spain, while he chose an apartment there for us to settle into together.

And so, one afternoon in August, three years after that second date, I stood in the rain outside the taxi that had taken me from the tiny Pau airport to the car park outside Michael's office. We transferred my luggage over to our new car so that Michael could bring it to our apartment after work. He spoke over my head to the taxi driver (easy with my five-foot-two frame), discussing in French where the driver could drop me off next to explore my new town.

Then he looked at me. 'Do you really want to go exploring in this rain? If you like I could give you the key, and you could just go straight home.'

Home, to a place I'd never even seen.

THE CAFÉ

I knew Michael wanted to show me the apartment himself, and anyway, I was eager to explore my new French town, even in the rain. 'No, that's okay,' I said. 'I can find a café if I want to be dry.'

Michael's shoulders dropped with relief that I wouldn't be judging our new home in his absence. He lifted my suitcase to take inside, and told the driver, 'Place Clemenceau, alors.'

He looked down at me. 'Welcome to Pau! I'll phone you when I've finished work so you can tell me where to meet you.' We kissed, and I climbed back into the taxi.

I had studied the map enough to know that Place Clemenceau was the main square in the centre of town, surrounded by shops and cafés. I also knew that the town was just an hour from the Pyrenees, and that Michael already enjoyed going to the Irish bar on the boulevard that offered a dramatic vista across to the mountain range. But that was all I knew. Otherwise, Pau was unknown and uncertain.

I had left behind Aberdeen, the Granite City. There's not much that's more solid, more certain, than granite. Almost all the buildings there were of the heavy, impenetrable stone quarried from the surrounding landscape. In fact, I had grown up in stone. The yellow sandstone of the house where I grew up, the red sandstone of Glasgow tenements…most of Scotland was stone-built. Those buildings had a permanence and a certitude that only stone could afford, like they had emerged from the ground itself, like they were part of the land.

Now, I had pulled up the roots I had dug into Aberdeen's granite foundation. Driving from Michael's office at the edge of Pau, through streets of squat concrete-rendered houses and modern apartment buildings, I wondered if I would ever feel grounded here. I dismissed the thought quickly, knowing that my decision to say 'yes' to this adventure was a no-brainer. Michael's job offer had come just as we were planning our wedding, and after a decade of teaching, I was ready for a break. I had the chance to take three years out and live in France, bankrolled by Michael's company to study French, eat baguettes, and travel around Europe. What more could I need?

Closer to the centre of town, I glimpsed older, more historic buildings, a charming boulangerie, and that view of the mountains through the rain. The driver pulled in between a car park entrance and a bank, and I paid him with crisp new euro notes. Holiday currency. I climbed out under grey skies and popped open my umbrella.

Place Clemenceau was a wide-open, elegant space, although not particularly historic, its surrounding buildings a mix of old and new facades. I dodged a car entering the ramp to the underground car park, and crossed the smooth paving towards the department store Galeries Lafayette, passing a large water fountain. Even in the rain, delighted small children were splashing through the jets of water that sporadically jumped out of the ground next to the fountain. The square was busy this Monday afternoon, with people hurrying between shops, or back to the office, or to meet someone at a café terrace. But so far, Place Clemenceau was an unfamiliar, unimpressive, grey town square, clouds reflecting in its puddles. The typically rainy town was not offering me its best first impression.

I couldn't explore too far, knowing that I would have to be able to explain to Michael where to meet me later. As I browsed in Galeries Lafayette and Sephora, the rain intensified, so I retreated to the nearest café, the one that was about to be my new favourite hangout.

Outside, a row of tables for two huddled under an awning; inside was narrow and long, with booths at the back on a raised area. I manoeuvred between tables with my dripping umbrella, awkwardly trying to avoid getting people wet. By the time I'd ordered a glass of *vin de table rouge*, the awkwardness was gone, and instead of taking my book out, I sat back to savour the moment.

A glass cabinet at the side near the entrance displayed croissants and pain au chocolats (I'd soon learn to order *une chocolatine* instead, in this corner of France) and elaborate glazed pâtisseries, laden with cream, fruit, or both. There were prepared sandwiches: half baguettes filled generously with jambon fromage or jambon beurre, poking from their waxed paper wraps. On top of the cabinet, small baskets of portioned baguettes waited for staff to reflexively place them on the table of anyone ordering food. The 'salads' on the menu listed rich elements like toast au chèvre, lardons, slices of duck.

The waiter – the manager, perhaps – knowingly indulged my awkward French as he brought the pichet of wine, but not knowing that he would become part of the origin story of my life in Pau. Over the following five years I'd be back here with friends, or visiting family, ordering a meat- and cheese-laden salad, and he would always be there. I'd point him out with a discreet whisper: 'He was the first person to serve me a drink in France.' And he would show no sign of recognising me, but was always ready to respond in English, no matter how much my French had improved in the meantime.

That first day, though, I relished the novelty of it all. I sipped my wine, living my new French life, at the perfect table, in the perfect café, with the perfect waiter, watching the rain fall outside, and thought nothing of sacrifice, or losing my independence or career path, or my life's purpose, or anything to do with the future. This moment, this was what my new life looked like.

Eventually, Michael's phone call broke my Gallic trance, and I told him I was at 'Le Cristal'. He dropped off the car and my luggage at the apartment then met me there. He suggested his new favourite place for dinner, which was on the way to our apartment.

'Lead the way,' I said. 'You're the one who knows where we're going.'

***

We ate burgers and drank beers and got pleasantly boozy in holiday mode, even if it was a Monday. 'Le Garage' would be our local, I discovered in the few minutes it took to walk 'home'.

I frowned as we left behind the older, more characterful part of the *centre-ville*. We certainly lived close enough to the action to make the most of our new life, but we passed by historic streets full of charm to get here. We walked up a dead-end street where Michael opened a gate just before the *parc des chiens* – the dog park, which, I later learned, could just as easily translate to 'dog toilet'.

We stood in front of an unremarkable modern apartment building.

'It's not the perfect location, but it was by far the best option they offered me,' Michael said. 'Anyway, inside is much nicer, honestly.'

'Don't worry, it all looks great!' I said, the pitch of my voice rising a little too high. I looked up at the soulless white building, part of a ring of late-twentieth-century development that swept across this part of town, and swallowed my disappointment. It didn't look French at all.

THE LIFT

T here was lots to love about our top floor two-bedroom apartment. After stepping off the elevator and across the threshold, I said what every one of our friends and family over the next three years would say on their first visit: 'Oh, it's *actually* really nice!' Floor-to-ceiling windows filled the living room with light and gave onto a wraparound balcony with a view of the Pyrenees (and the dog toilet, and a mysterious convent-style compound that had no name on the map, but had a statue of the Madonna that seemed to watch us whenever we stepped outside). We roasted in that apartment the first summer, because I wouldn't close the shutters during the day. What northern European would willingly shut out that much glorious southern light? We were close to the centre-ville. Our lounge was all curves and modernity and white walls – it would make an impressive party backdrop. We had a decent-sized kitchen, and a second bedroom for guests, which was where I set up a desk for studying French.

Then again, as with any rental, there was plenty I didn't love: a bathroom lined with dated blue-and-brown tiles, from wall to wall to ceiling to floor; minimal kitchen storage, although this apartment had more fitted cabinets than any others Michael had seen, since the French mostly still favoured traditional freestanding kitchen furniture at that time; the separate toilet, my first of many tiny, depressing separate toilets. In French homes, the toilet was almost always separate from the bathroom. There were hygiene reasons, I supposed, but I found it uncomfortably confining, like sitting in a windowless cupboard, and just another room to clean full of awkward corners and crannies. Frequently, there was no sink in there either, so I had to carry my besmirched hands into the bathroom to wash.

The lift (elevator) was right beside our apartment door. I can summon the sound of it now, so that it echoes between my ears, but it's at its most potent when I think I hear it outside my head, when some other movement around me momentarily sounds exactly like it, and I'm back in that apartment. As the lift made its way up six floors, I could hear it from any room. Before long, I was counting the seconds, so that I would know if it was about to stop on the floor below, or coming all the way up. I tuned into the hissing zoom as it moved up the building, followed by a muffled clunk if it stopped on our floor. And if it did, there was a one in three chance that the door to our apartment would click open next, and Michael would return home.

I'm not a puppy or a young child, but that sound – echoed or imagined – still provokes in me that sense of smallness. It was the sound of my husband returning home. To me. As if I was waiting there, aproned and domesticated, or lonely and aimless, until he was with me.

I know that wasn't the case. Yet, sometimes that sound brought deep relief, or comfort.

The first weeks of my time in Pau, it turned out, were not all baguettes, pichets of wine, and hours of café life.

They were waking up in a strange place with Michael already off to work early. My days comprised unpacking the shipment, and sorting out the internet – in French, with a cheque book. I had to learn how to drive on the 'wrong' side of the road, and, more importantly, how to drive like a French person, with Michael urging me from the passenger seat: 'Go now! No, don't let them through. Be more aggressive! What are you waiting for?'

Other days found me translating ingredients from a dictionary before I wrote the shopping list, which was as time-consuming as it sounds, but not as simple. 'Self-raising flour' became *farine auto-levante* – even with my basic French grammar I knew that probably wasn't right. Then I'd venture into various unfamiliar supermarkets, only to find completely different products on the shelves: half a dozen types of bread flour, none of them giving any indication of raising ability.

I'd get going slowly in the morning, finally decide to head in to town for a walk or to look at the shops, but then realise that it was already nearly midday, so the shops would be closed.

I considered going furniture shopping. Michael's company supplied furnishings as part of the relocation package, so before he moved in, he had chosen from a photocopied document with low-resolution pictures of a basic selection of sofas, dining tables, lighting, etc. I later heard a rumour that the 'catalogue' contents were overstock from already-cheap-and-cheerful French furniture chain Fly (think less-chic Ikea, or if you're in Denmark, exactly-as-chic Jysk). We ended up with a brown velour corner sofa, a sideboard and dining table of indeterminate brown wood, and other uninspiring and insubstantial pieces.

I'd been a nester all my life, carefully curating spaces from my childhood bedroom, to my room in halls at university (like a dorm), to every flat share, and finally to my very own home. I wanted to do the same here, but this time we wouldn't be staying, and we already had what we needed, even if it wasn't ideal. I couldn't bring myself to make the investment for a temporary nest.

The worst of our acquired furnishings was the cream shag rug. This shag wasn't the plush, soft, luxurious type of 1970s glamour accessory. It was more ropey than fluffy, with ends always coming adrift from the weave, and impossible to keep clean, crumbs emerging from deep in the polyester forest long after that particular snack had been eaten. I hated that rug.

I would regularly announce to Michael, while vacuuming, or feeling the ropey strands between my toes on a hot day, 'I hate that rug.'

'Why don't we just replace it then?'

'What's the point? Why spend money on something when we're not staying here permanently? It would just be wasteful if we didn't keep it after we moved.'

So the rug stayed beneath our feet. I restricted myself to making use of the bare minimum of kitchen equipment, because there was no extra space in the cupboards, and I repaired a collapsing drawer in the bedroom over and over again. We didn't want to invest anything beyond the essential in a space that we wouldn't be in long term. We already had nice things in storage in the attic of

Michael's flat back in Aberdeen. As far as I was concerned, we would go back to those things in three years' time. Until then, we would make do.

THE SOURCE

The realisation that my French skills were not quite what I thought they were was the most disconcerting feeling of all.

Michael, just learning French, didn't seem to care. 'I just use the words I've got, and when they run out, I point! Or I use English until the person in the boulangerie figures it out.'

But I was too proud to wing it, to muddle through. Before any interaction, I would prepare for the conversation, either mentally, or with a dictionary and pen and paper.

I'd arrived in Pau with all the confidence of the native-English speaker who has learned a little of another language, which is to say, more confidence than I deserved. French was one of my top subjects at school, and I'd even taken classes at university. Fifteen years later, that knowledge had become very well hidden.

It was a strange and completely new experience, to not be freely able to communicate. I couldn't just smile and point and gesture. I couldn't bear the thought of walking in somewhere and having to so obviously display my lack of knowledge, lack of language.

For an English teacher, a self-proclaimed expert in the English language, someone who had gone through life able to communicate with articulacy, able to express myself freely and without fear of rejection or being misunderstood, it felt like I had lost a part of me. I was no longer fully functioning, like I'd lost a limb, I would dramatically tell myself.

I'd arrived in France thinking I would spend my days visiting *le marché*, and people-watching from street cafés, before returning to our apartment to create a home full of French chic and meals full of Gallic flavour. But I didn't know how to get to that. So I did spend those days aimlessly, flicking between the BBC news channel and French TV, searching fruitlessly for entertainment in English with subtitles – a rare discovery, since almost all imported TV and film in France was dubbed. Trying to watch French TV just added to my sense of aimlessness by making me feel stupid.

And then the sound of the lift would murmur its way up the building, and my boredom, my waiting for something to do, would be over.

But I was losing my voice.

***

I hadn't made a plan for my three years in France. Maybe I'd get a teaching job; maybe we would have a baby, since I was on a career break anyway.

Meanwhile, in those first weeks, I was hanging around waiting to hear from Michael's company about the language lessons they would provide.

I had to wait for Michael to come home each evening, and ask, 'Have you heard from HR yet? About my French classes?' If there was no news I would say, 'Can you ask them about it tomorrow?' And he would try, but perhaps the next day they wouldn't be in the office when he was free, or he would be too busy, between getting his job done, his own language classes, a workplace culture workshop. A couple of days later I would ask again, feeling whiny, and wheedling, and hating being dependent on him. Eventually I said, 'Just give me the number for the HR office, I'll call them myself.' I wanted to take control for myself of this one little, crucial, thing, but I said, 'You've obviously got more important things to deal with, let me deal with this and it'll be off your plate.'

'No, that's not the right way to do it,' he said, 'I'm figuring out how to deal with the office politics. It has to go through me. It'll only annoy people if someone's wife starts hassling them.'

The days dragged on like that, as I felt my autonomy dissolve into thin air. For the first time in twenty years, my plans were beyond my control, beyond my agency. And, I thought, there was nothing I could do about it.

Since my teens, I had been used to advocating confidently for myself. Whether pushing for my subject choices in high school, or calling the university admissions office to organise my postgraduate study, or showing up for job interviews, or applying for the mortgage to buy my first flat, or pitching my boss for professional development, auditioning to join a theatre company, travelling alone, or even getting my profile on match.com to take control of my own love life...I was used to going straight to the source. It had been a very long time since I let anyone else arrange something on my behalf. I had the freedom of not waiting to be invited.

But now, I was denied access to the source. I wondered if I would ever get invited back in to my own life.

Eventually, I got an email from someone in HR, listing a few options. I replied, choosing a centrally located language school that offered lessons twice a week. But I was disappointed that something more intensive wasn't on offer.

Then I waited again, for confirmation of the details and a start date.

'Have you heard anything more about my French lessons? Do you know if they got my email?'

'No,' he sighed. 'I'll try to follow up tomorrow...if I have time.'

Late one afternoon, about a month after arriving in Pau, instead of the sound of the lift, it was the sound of the phone ringing that interrupted my channel surfing. And the call was actually for me.

'I am calling to confirm for you the French lessons,' said the company HR rep. 'But, it is a surprise to me that you do not choose the university classes. You are available all day, yes? No children?'

My heart leapt. 'I can go to university classes? You didn't give me that option in the email before.'

'Really? I must have forgotten. But yes, there they have classes for twenty hours a week. They are for all different levels. But you do not get private lessons. It is bigger classes, maybe fifteen students.'

'Yes! Yes please. That's what I want to do. Sign me up. Please!'

'I can do that...oh, but the placement test is tomorrow morning. Maybe it is too late–'

'No! I'll be there. Give me the address and please tell them I'm coming!'

I noted the location, and went down in the lift to get my brand-new bike from its stand in the bike room at the bottom of the building. Off I went on a recce, to make sure I wouldn't be late the following morning, cutting through the dog park/toilet, navigating an enormous roundabout along with French drivers eager to get home, and discovering the modern but leafy campus of the Université de Pau et des Pays d'Adour, where my new life would begin.

The following morning, I waited, early for once, in the lobby of the languages building. Grinning with all the uncool enthusiasm of a mature student, I joined at least 150 other students from all over the world, as we filed into a lecture theatre to complete the test that would determine the class for our level.

I launched into lessons and homework for my 'Elementaire' class, exhilarated by my return to daily student life. Truthfully, throughout much of my twenties I had missed the sense of community that student life had represented for me – adulthood had seemed to mean fewer friends, less spontaneity, and, what's worse, less learning. After ten years of teaching, the joy of sitting on the other side of the desk, of showing up daily and just absorbing what I could learn, letting myself grow with none of the responsibility, was delicious.

I made quick progress. My earlier learning returned so naturally with daily use, I barely noticed. I skipped a level and by the third trimester I was in the 'Perfectionnement' class, with less language learning and more immersion through studying other subjects.

In the literature class, we all had to present a French novel, and I chose one that really marked the progress I had made. After reading extracts in class from contemporary authors, as well as some French classics, curiosity sent me to re-read *Le Silence de la Mer* by Vercors, which I'd first read in high school. It's a short novel, a novella really, with simple language. But try telling that to a class of sixteen-year-olds with a raft of other exams to study for and no interest in the *not*-so-simple *passé simple*. Back then, I had a foggy grasp of the plot.

This time, I discovered a story that was moving in its simplicity, with spare prose that nevertheless told every nuance of a moving relationship. Best of all, I discovered I could now read French without that fog of misunderstanding.

When I presented it to the class in Pau, the teacher gave an oh-so-Gallic eyebrow raise of judgement at my emphasis in the phrase 'j'ai *dû* lire ce livre à l'école (I *had* to read this book at school)'. But I explained how my new depth of knowledge had brought fresh understanding and enjoyment to the book. Then I got to show off to my classmates with my English-teacher-level literary analysis of its prose and characterisation.

I had found my voice again, for now.

THE REARRANGED CHAIRS

I t was hard to imagine what our social life in Pau would look like before it began. I broke away from one of my aimless, channel surfing days in the first couple of weeks by phoning a number that Michael had given me: the wife of a Scottish colleague. The couple had arrived around the same time as us.

It probably took a couple of days of me looking at the digits on the sticky note, reaching for the phone, then putting the handset back in the base, before I actually dialled the number. She answered quickly.

'Hello?' There was chatter in the background.

'Hello, is this Eve? This is Catriona. Our husbands are trying to hook us up!' I cringed at my eager attempt at humour.

'Of course, Paul said he'd passed on my number. Hi!'

'Is this a good time for you to talk?'

'Yes, it's fine. I'm just in Fly, trying to find some decent bookshelves that don't cost a bloody fortune!' Her voice moved away from the mouthpiece at the sound of a toddler's plea. 'Put that down, darling.' I was already impressed by her next-level decision making and multi-tasking.

Eve invited me for coffee the following day, and I walked out of town in the fierce August heat to their sprawling suburban house, where she offered home bakes and described their life in Angola, where they'd moved from. I didn't have much to say about my adventures in French TV. She was about my age, but a parent, and a more experienced expat. She exuded confidence and mastery of all it meant to be a wife abroad, filling a home with furniture and organising play dates for her daughter. I was absolutely drawn to her friendliness and honesty and expertise, and we're still in touch today, but as we walked together back to our apartment, her pushing the buggy over awkward French pavements, manoeuvring around the ubiquitous *caca de chien,* I felt she was out of my expat league – more grown-up than I could imagine becoming.

Another option was the established community of anglophones in the area, who'd formed a society organising social events and sharing useful information in English. I'd found their website before arriving, and kept an eye on their event calendar.

About a month after we moved, I dutifully signed us up for their annual summer barbecue, and dragged Michael along, against his better judgement.

'Listen,' I said, 'it's all very well for you, working for a large company at an office campus full of international employees. But I need to meet more people!'

I had an address, directions, and the map of the region Michael had bought when he first picked up our car. (In 2009, in-car GPS was a thing. But we liked reading maps and were not interested in forking out extra cash for a machine that would tell us where to go, when a map would give us the fun of unfolding and exploring the world around us.)

Because it was another rainy day – there were many of those in this mountain region – the event had been moved at the last minute to a farm property with a large barn-turned-function room, which turned out to be nearly an hour away including 'exploration' time, up a country road in the Pyrenean foothills that surround Pau. By the time we arrived at the remote farm, Michael was not any happier to have given up his Sunday afternoon for getting lost in the Béarn, just to meet a group of strangers he would probably never see again. But, in my wilful optimism, I had visions of finding a group of lively thirty-somethings just like me, who would be fascinated to learn about us, and our new adventure, and me, in all my intriguing uniqueness.

We parked on a patch of muddy grass set aside for cars for the day, and made our way towards what looked like the entrance. Sure enough, there was some-body standing behind a trestle table, taking our names and payment. A smell of smoke and grim perseverance drifted from round a corner, where volunteers were grilling under a gazebo, diving through the rain in and out of a kitchen for plates of food and utensils. It all felt very familiar, very British-summertime, and suddenly I wondered if that was really what I wanted.

Inside, there were long tables lined up along each side of a large room, with members chatting among the piles of paper plates. There were a few small children running back and forth across the room, so there must have been at least some people around our age. But the overwhelming impression was of middle-aged familiarity, a roomful of retirees who all seemed to know each other already. As the two of us stood uncertainly, wondering where to place ourselves, and with me defiantly ignoring the low, barely audible grumbles from Michael, a smiling rosy-cheeked woman who'd been floating between the seated participants approached us with eager enthusiasm.

'Hello! You're new, I think? I haven't met you before!' I could tell she was hungrily taking in our relative youth and the freshness of our blood.

We introduced ourselves. 'We've only been here a few weeks,' I said. 'We don't know anyone here.'

'Ah, I hear a Scottish accent! Well, there's someone Scottish over there, let me introduce you!' She swept us over to a table and sat us opposite an even-younger-than-us, fresh-faced, smiling brunette. Heather had arrived a few months before us for a teaching job at the small international school. Younger and much cooler than us, she was feeling just as out of place as we were, I realised later, probably more so.

Although we didn't feel like we fit in, everyone there was friendly and enthusiastic to see some new faces – until they weren't. I soon spotted a pattern to the conversations. After introducing themselves (a Brit retiring to rural France, a family retreating from the fast-paced modern world to renovate a farmhouse and home-school their children, empty nesters setting up a B&B and gîte business...) they would be interested in hearing why we were there, until we mentioned Michael's company. 'Ah...' they would say, fixing the friendly smile but with their voice dropping a little. 'So you're not staying long term.' Then the conversation would quickly peter out and we would have to turn to someone else to avoid looking like complete wallflowers.

That was my first taste of how our serial expat life would affect the way we formed relationships. Some people preferred to invest their social energy in people they knew were sticking around, relationships that would have staying power. And I suspected that some of these 'lifers' probably had bitter experience of short-term expats like us becoming friends then moving on, or realising they had more in common with other frequent movers, their presence fading after that first enthusiasm.

But those were the people I hadn't found yet. We trudged back to the car, Michael working hard to bite his tongue. Eventually, back on the road, under still grey and droopy skies, he caved. 'I told you so!'

***

The following week, my French lessons began, and I started making connections with some of my (mostly much younger) classmates.

One day, after cycling back to the apartment from my afternoon class, I looked around the bright living room, with its spectacular balcony and views. It would be perfect for a party. We could shift the angle of the sofa to open up the room more, push the table into the corner and pile it with food, set up a bar on the sideboard, and rearrange the dining chairs around the room.

We just didn't have anyone to invite yet.

A couple of weeks later, though, our people emerged. Michael's company organised an 'international soirée' for new arrivals.

As we arrived at the function suite in the glamorous Palais Beaumont, we learned that the foodie-themed event included a competitive element. Coming from my teaching background, these were my first steps into the world of corporate hospitality and team-building, since Michael had mostly worked offshore during our dating life. My eyes widened at the lavish spread of food and drink at stations around the room, and I walked a little taller to see the amount of spending and preparation that had gone in to welcoming us to Pau. It was nice to feel appreciated – I could get used to this!

The event organisers split couples up into different teams, to maximise mingling. I found myself with a group of people I hadn't met before. I was drawn to the girl standing beside me in a tartan skirt and black heels. An organiser handed out our team aprons for the evening's programme of cooking and food challenges. As we all tied our apron strings, I caught her eye with a nervous smile and said something about being 'useless in the kitchen'. Her face broke into a warm, cheerful grin as she said, 'I know, right? I hope the rest of this team know what they're doing!' We laughed together, introduced ourselves, and my new friend Laurie and I relaxed into the activities like co-conspirators, catching one another's attention for a cheeky eye roll whenever someone seemed to take the egg-whisking challenge too seriously.

During a break, I said, 'I better catch up with my other half.' We each drifted towards our respective partners, and discovered they'd already homed in on each other. In fact, Laurie's boyfriend, George, was the person Michael had spotted as we entered the room and whispered to me, 'That guy – he's Scottish. Guaranteed.' George's rebellious and very un-French suit-and-sneaks look had marked him out, and his dour, cynical sense of humour squarely identified him as being from Aberdeen as much as his familiar, lyrical accent. This down-to-earth Canadian-Scottish partnership became our first ever official couple friends.

A week after the cooking soirée, we met up with Laurie for drinks, and she invited a colleague along whom she promised was 'Totally awesome!' with her customary generous enthusiasm. (Her text message included a lot more exclamation marks.) I perched at the bar of Le Garage, pint (well, demi-litre) of beer in hand, Michael beside me, waiting for the others to arrive. Suddenly a perky breathless voice was at my elbow. 'You're Michael aren't you? I've seen you at the office.' She turned to me. 'Hi, I'm Hannah. Oh my goodness, sorry I'm late!' And then she probably told some chaotic tale of everything that had happened to her, or her cat, or her car, between leaving work that day and arriving at the bar. Hannah worked in IT at the same company and was also from Aberdeen. Adding to her ever-smiling perkiness was the fact that she looked a good ten years younger than her thirtyish years. Her chaotic cheerfulness led many to underestimate her, but actually she had a powerful expertise in her subject and was a headstrong decision-maker.

In late October, Laurie and George hosted a flat warming party at their apartment by the river, and there, our new family grew further. It was early in the skiing season, so Michael and I had hit the slopes that day with snowboards. As impressive as that sounds, it had all been a bit overambitious. Michael had learned to snowboard years before, during his time as a ski bum in the Canadian Rockies, and was eager to hit the Pyrenean slopes. I was equally eager to show him I could be the cool girl who would take advantage of living near the mountains, and become a boarder along with her husband. We didn't book any lessons, and Michael showed me the ropes in my hired gear.

But I was the teacher in the family, not him. With each thud of my coccyx onto the snow and ice of the beginner slope, he couldn't explain how I should change my form, and just repeated the same instructions over again. The freedom of the grownup runs was calling him, and his irritation grew.

It ended in tears. We were badly in need of a party.

In the small galley kitchen of Laurie and George's stylish flat, I listened at length to Ben. He had recently arrived from Calgary, and his fellow Canadian invited him along so that he could meet some more of the international community. Tall and lean with a booming voice and expressive eyebrows, Ben had that North American confidence in talking about himself – an assurance that he himself was an interesting topic of conversation. I could only aspire to that level of confidence. And he wasn't entirely wrong – it was fascinating to me the way he insisted he had a 'girl in every port' – in all the places he'd lived or visited for work, he'd met someone who could've been the one, whom he'd had to let down gently. But his bravado faded into something adorably sincere when he described another girl. There was someone back home in Canada, who he'd known a long time. He smiled coyly, endearingly self-aware. 'There's nothing serious, but...I'm kinda hopeful. I'm trying to persuade her to come out here and visit. But she has her own stuff going on.' He looked down and swirled his beer. 'Well, we'll see.'

A few months later, Ben invited Michael and me to go bowling, saying, 'I have a friend staying with me.' We met them in the car park of the bowling alley. Ben had persuaded Mel to take a break from her job in Canada to come and visit him – and it was going well. Tall and dark-haired, she wore a sexy green wrap dress, accessorised with such fun and confidence that I immediately developed a massive friend crush. I thought she was out of my league, but luckily Ben won her over and she moved to France.

That was the group that formed in those early months in Pau, and which became our first expat family. There were other important friends too, from Germany, Venezuela, Australia, England, Romania...But the Scottish-Canadian clan of Michael and me, Laurie and George, Hannah, Ben, and Mel is the family that became a core friendship group for years to come.

Almost all my most vivid and treasured memories of our time in Pau include that family, between nights out in the Galway Irish pub, on the Boulevard des Pyrénées with its mountain views, and tripping through the streets on midsummer night for the Fête de la Musique, plastic pint glasses in hand, finding performances round every corner. We even went horse trekking in the mountains one spring morning, followed by a *casse-croute*, a shared picnic, with supplies from the local market.

So I got my party moments: friends piling together into one another's small apartments, moving the furniture around to fit as many international friends as possible into one room to share our cultural rituals. In Ben and Mel's apartment, they somehow squeezed three dining tables into one room and strategically disguised them with tablecloths to make one long banqueting table where a crowd gathered for Canadian Thanksgiving dinner. Another wine-loving friend gathered us in his very old city apartment, above a courtyard hidden behind the main cobbled shopping street, for wine-tasting challenges. It was up a staircase that felt like a challenge in itself, with its two-hundred-year-old structure tilting acutely to one side. It was even more of a challenge to descend at the end of the night.

At our place, we hosted one particularly memorable Burns Supper: forty people somehow crammed into our living room, with the table pushed to one side and the sofa pushed up against the windows and dining chairs lined up around the room. The flowing whisky helped everyone find enough space, while I juggled the heating up of enough haggis and tatties, and only a small amount of *navets* – the closest French veg I could find to turnips to make a cross-cultural version of 'neeps'. Music blared, lamps lit up every corner, and I had every ring on the stove going while I heated haggis in the oven.

Then everything went black.

Ben's voice boomed out in the dark, and I could hear the delighted teasing smile in his words. 'Hey, Turners! Get the power back on! What have you done dudes?' But it was he who figured out that we had overloaded the system and blown the fuse, who found the fuse box, and got us cooking again. I slowed down the process, and after several more whiskies, everyone finally got fed. That stressful part done with, I moved on from red wine and tore into the whisky myself, my body absorbing it all a little too greedily as the adrenaline subsided. I remember that somehow we managed ceilidh dancing up-and-down, or side-to-side at least, between the sofa and the table, on the shag pile rug, in the wee small hours. And then I remember it morphed into Breton dancing, its Celtic style so similar to a ceilidh that it inspired our friends from north-west France to teach us their idiosyncratic moves too. Unfortunately, I also remember the next part, when the adrenaline and wine and whisky had their revenge.

That family rooted us in our new life, and keeps us rooted still, no matter the distance.

THE LOBBY

Towards the end of our first year in France, my bonus year as a full-time student was coming to an end. After four hours of lessons a day, plus homework and presentations and long lunches with my classmates, I could once again claim 'good at French' as part of my identity. Never mind that I spent my time in an international community with people who were already fluent English speakers as their second or third language, and also adding French to their repertoire. Like so many anglophones, I cherished my one great language-learning achievement.

I was pretty smug about my French. I was *nickel, merci,* and throwing around idioms after the first time I heard them. I wasn't fluent, but I was ready to handle myself in most everyday situations.

One day, I arrived back at our apartment building, shopping bags in hand, and fumbled the key out of my pocket to open the door to the building. Once inside the cool shade of the wide open lobby, I noticed one of my neighbours was fishing her mail out of her letterbox.

Like most French apartment buildings, ours had a wall of letterboxes in the lobby, one for each apartment. Ours were in a separate room screened off by slatted wooden panels. Some parcels would fit in them, but we would be lucky to get anything bigger or heavier delivered on time. I would often discover that *le facteur* had left a postcard in the letterbox about a parcel to be collected at the depot, rather than buzz me to come down, as they were supposed to do.

Our neighbours included quite a few elderly residents. This lady was the one who lived below us, who had an amazing array of plants on her balcony, and who, even at her stage of life, embodied that effortless French chic that is more than a stereotype. Elegant clothes, coordinated outfits, coiffed hair, and always put together, even just for a trip downstairs in the *ascenseur*. She was standing upright and poised in front of her mailbox, flipping through some envelopes. In my scruffy jeans and T-shirt, I tried blowing messy strands of hair out of my face, my hands full with shopping bags. I squeezed myself through the heavy building door before it could slam shut on me, and awkwardly rearranged the bags before one of them could drop and spill its contents on the white tile floor. I silently rehearsed some French small talk, knowing that I was unlikely to escape a ride in the lift together with my intimidating neighbour.

She left the mailbox area, and we said the obligatory polite 'Bonjour!' to one another as we both approached the lift. Waiting for the doors to open, she smiled. 'Il fait beau aujourd'hui.' In all countries and languages, the weather makes for reliable small talk.

'Oui,' I said. 'Ça fait du bien quand le soleil brille!' Wow, I was pleased with that one. It feels good when the sun shines. Her smile broadened, and I felt the glow of her approval shining on me, too.

The lift door opened, and she gestured to me to go before her. I couldn't possibly. And I had another expression to practise. 'Non non Madame, vas-y!' I said, cheerfully indicating that she should enter first. She did, and I followed, and as the door slid shut in front of us, the air suddenly became chilly. That beam of her approval was gone. There would be no more small talk.

I kept a nervous smile fixed on my face until we reached the fifth floor. 'Bonne soirée!' I eagerly sang out as she left.

Her politesse was reflexive, but there was no eye contact when she tossed back her reply. 'Oui, bonne soirée madame.'

About half an hour later, my stomach suddenly lurched when I realised what I had done. *Quel horreur!* I had *tutoyéed* my elderly French neighbour! When I told her to 'go ahead' into the lift, I had used the *vas* form of the verb *aller* that would go with the informal *tu*, when I should have said 'Allez-y'. And with such an informal expression in the first place!

Our relationship was never quite the same after I had broken that cardinal rule, although it didn't knock my confidence too much – at least I had figured it out for myself.

Mind you, I was speaking French, but I had no interest in *being* French. The *Version Française* held no appeal for me.

Since the French dub almost all imported films, going to the cinema meant scouring listings for screenings labelled VO – *version originale* (or VOST – *version originale sous-titrée*), which meant a film showing in its original language with French subtitles. Everything else was VF – dubbed over to make a *version française*. Luckily for my film geek side, there was one art-house cinema in Pau, Le Mélies, which valued VO films.

After the honeymoon period of French living had worn off, the *version originale* was all I wanted, and not just in the cinema. There was so much about the VF of my life in Pau that I wanted to see past, and just stick with the VO – the version that would fit with my idea of normal.

I missed the certainty of granite, the solid base Aberdeen had given me for so long. Instead, most of the buildings around Pau were brick, or more likely concrete, rendered and whitewashed. Only the very centre of Pau, around the historic chateau, had a cluster of buildings from before the mid-twentieth century. The town was beautiful, but its architecture represented a lack of permanence to me. The lack of front doors disconcerted me. There was something so solid and British about a front door – even in tenement buildings they were solidly there in the middle of the building. Access to French homes was often hidden round the side, or accessed from the building's rear car park. In this town, finding a way in was elusive.

I couldn't figure out the French shopping experience. The country was famous for its luxury brands, of course, but beyond the designer boutiques, the only alternatives seemed to be pile-em-high fast fashion, too cheap and flimsy. I missed M&S and Next and other UK brands for mid-price, reasonable quality. And shopping for vitamins, shampoo, first aid, and cosmetics meant going to four different places. That didn't make sense to me after a lifetime of filling a Boots basket with all those things. It turned out the British high street was a luxury I never knew I'd miss until I did. *The version française* didn't measure up.

Much as I liked French café life, I wished for a *version originale* of a long and lingering coffee while I sat there, instead of the tiny, sip-and-go, bitter espressos that were on offer as a *version française*. And then there was the language: hierarchical, rigid, and bound to get me into trouble with the neighbours. No, I just wanted to live as my *version originale*, thank you very much. Which made for a lot of discomfort, given that I was immersed in a French version of my life.

I stubbornly resisted adapting. As far as I was concerned, I would go 'home' to Scotland, sooner or later. Eventually, I would return to what was normal. Every difference I encountered, every cultural challenge that wasn't quite right, that represented something 'other', was like a grain of sand in the oyster shell, working away at me – but not creating a pearl, just constant low-level irritation. Whether it was the bureaucracy, the inflexible opening hours, the illegible cursive handwriting, or the dog poop on every pavement, I only had to tolerate these things, because they were not my normal, they were only temporary, and one day, I'd get *back* to normal.

In our apartment, the temporary shag rug remained, the crumbs embedded in its fibres as irritating as the grains of cultural sand. I would wrinkle my nose as I walked barefoot across the rug, and as I stepped over the dog poop on the narrow pavement. But it didn't matter, because this town and this country were not home. Home was a place north of here, a pin on the map, with longitude and latitude coordinates. That was the dwelling place of my normal, the place I would always fit in.

Of course, despite all that stubborn resistance, deep in my core I was being reshaped and redefined. Like a background process running unseen on a computer, my identity was adapting, changing me from a person from one place to a person of many places. But it was only years later that I fully embraced my true *version française*.

THE DECAFF COFFEE

In the spring, after we'd been living in Pau for seven months, I heard that the fledgling international school was looking for a new English teacher. When we first met Marcus, the school's history teacher, at a party, and he heard about my experience, he almost begged me to apply. 'Please! We need an English teacher! I am so fed up trying to teach GCSE poetry.'

By this time Michael and I were ready to try for a baby, but who knew how long that would take? And I fully intended to be a working parent with whatever opportunity presented itself. But it was spring, I still had plenty of time left to enjoy my course, and although I expected to go back to teaching at some point, I wasn't in a hurry to give up my relaxed days and freedom from working.

Michael was keen to encourage me otherwise. 'Even if it's for starting a job in September, you should reach out to the school now, and let them know how experienced you are.' I knew he was always conscious of the career I'd left behind, and that I missed the independence I'd been used to.

'That makes sense, but I'm not even convinced that I want to get straight back to work this year. And then I would need to learn about a different curriculum.'

'Those are just details. There's no harm in getting in touch – that's not the same as making a decision! Throw your hat in the ring.'

And sure enough, by the summer, I had a job. The school was growing, and had already hired a full-time English teacher who was new to the role. The head teacher hired me to help establish the curriculum for older students. The offer was ideal: part-time work with small classes of international kids, and the rest of the time to enjoy our life in France.

(Mind you, Michael's encouragement did backfire on him. He was used to letting his colleagues take vacation days during their children's school holidays. 'What if we go to Spain for a week near the end of September?'

'Um, sorry, no can do. Remember when you encouraged me to apply for a teaching job? Only school holidays for us now!')

Meanwhile, as the summer passed, we were carefully counting weeks and months. Before long, I said to Michael, 'It's been a few days, I think we should check,' and we bought a pregnancy test at the pharmacy.

Michael fidgeted on the brown velour sofa, knee jiggling, waiting to find out if what he'd dreamed of for years would come to pass.

In our tiny toilet-cupboard, I did the deed with a mixture of hope and trepidation. I was excited about the decision we'd made to expand our family, and there was no reason to wait any longer, but I'd never been broody. For Michael and I to become parents together was one thing: a joyful expression of our love and partnership. But for me to become a 'mum', with all the added weight society added to that word, when I was already a dependent wife, was just a bit terrifying.

But I still had time to get used to the idea, I was sure. We'd only been trying for three months. I didn't know anyone my age who'd got pregnant that quickly.

I emerged with the test, and we watched it together.

I was pregnant.

Michael was overjoyed, and his elation was infectious. Our next adventure was beginning.

We made an appointment with an obstetrician. To my amazement, he instantly did a scan, and we could already hear the extra heartbeat of our new family member, our new little co-adventurer.

Michael was already a studious reader of pregnancy and baby books. He had questions primed for the doctor. 'So, she shouldn't eat any blue cheese now, is that right?'

I looked away and rolled my eyes – he was dubious of anything unpasteurised or mould-based at the best of times.

'Yes, that's right,' said the doctor, 'no unpasteurised dairy products. Also, be careful with salad – you have to be sure that it is very thoroughly washed. No uncooked meat. You can have a little wine, but no more alcohol than that.'

'What about coffee?' said Michael. I pursed my lips. He was a non-coffee-drinker too, highly sceptical of anyone's dependence on caffeine.

'Like the wine – just a little. One coffee a day is *bon*.'

I could enjoy that pleasure at least.

The very next day, I got ready to start my new job, racked with guilt even though it was too soon to change any plans. I poured my usual cup of coffee in the kitchen.

Michael stopped me. 'What are you doing?'

'The doctor said I can have one cup of coffee a day. This is my one cup.'

'No, I don't want you to have any! If less is good, then none is definitely better.'

I frowned. 'I'll get some decaff when I'm shopping later. But I'm having this one now. First day of a new job? I mean, come on...'

And on top of any normal first-day jitters, I was nervous to be starting work with a secret. Day two of a pregnancy was definitely too early for making announcements, especially to a group of people I'd literally just met, but I hated the idea that I was starting a brand new job already with a plan to take time off within months.

That first day, there were no lessons, just my new colleagues and I getting classrooms and resources ready for the start of term. My generous new boss took the teaching staff out for lunch at a nearby restaurant: a typical French workday lunch of a set three-course menu, with *pichets* of wine at the table.

As we filed in, I found myself sitting next to the Early Years teacher, who was visibly, heavily pregnant. There was the sound of a cork popping – we were to toast the new academic year with some champagne. My new colleague beside me refused the bubbles while I gingerly sipped at the small glass, having decided I would taste it rather than bring attention to the fact that I wasn't drinking it.

The waitress brought a starter of salad and uncooked charcuterie. Kate, my pregnant lunch companion, declined, and so did I.

Someone offered to pour wine for everybody. Kate declined, and so did I, gesturing that I still had champagne in the glass that I was sipping from painfully slowly.

After the main course came a portion of Roquefort – unpasteurised blue cheese, another banned food. Kate turned it down, and I cursed myself for having sat next to the most pregnant-looking person in the room, as I yet again declined the same thing as her. I squirmed in my seat, checking to see how much attention people were paying, and reached for another sip of champagne in the hope it would give me cover. Everything I loved most about French eating habits was working against me today.

But nobody really was paying much attention. I couldn't believe that at least Kate didn't figure it out that day; if she did, she never said.

I finally told my head teacher a few weeks later, just before the start of the October holiday, and to my relief she bounded out from behind her desk and gave me an overwhelming hug of congratulations. It was a relief, too, that the secret was out, and I could now relax into the anticipation of the adventure Michael and I were about to share.

THE CAR KEYS

Baby Cameron arrived two weeks early. On the Saturday before, Laurie hosted a baby shower for me at her apartment. Ben and Mel were getting married in Canada around the time of Cameron's due date, so we planned a bachelorette for Mel for the same night. The pastel-coloured, cupcake-focused afternoon gradually dissolved into a tequila-fuelled evening. Walking with Hannah, I made it as far as dinner at the Mexican restaurant along the road from Laurie's, hauling myself and my bump as we walked – I did not have a neat and elegant pregnancy.

I parted ways from the others after the meal, leaving them to make their way on to the bars and clubs of Pau. Michael was coming to pick me up. 'Where will you be standing?' he asked.

'I'll wait outside the restaurant. Don't worry – you won't be able to miss the eight-months-pregnant ball in an oversized sombrero.'

I was on maternity leave already, so after that weekend, I was ready to enjoy two guilt-free weeks of magazines and TV and just waiting. On Sunday Mel delivered the tower of cupcakes she'd made that were left over from the shower – too busy with presents and baby-themed games, I'd forgotten to even taste one on the day, so I was going to relish every one of them as I waited.

Late Tuesday morning I got into a bath, where I was tuning into a feeling of 'home' by listening to BBC Radio 4. The book of the week was a collection of Roald Dahl short stories, and I had never read that day's tale. I remember enjoying the new story, and looking forward to my afternoon of sweet treats and nothing to do. I never heard the end of that story to find out what the plot twist would be.

I had my own twist in the tale.

As I lay with my head back in the water, I felt some movement between my legs. Was my water breaking? If it was, I would have to get straight out of the bath. With my head still back, I lay still and gauged the movement. It had been too gentle a sensation to be waters breaking – I knew that would be a great flood, and I would be more aware of it, even in the bath. Reassured, I hauled myself carefully up to sit, and started shampooing my hair. But then I looked down. Blood was floating in the water between my legs and spreading to the rest of the bath. And it wasn't stopping. An icy chill crept up my spine. I tried to steady my breathing as I hauled myself up again, this time to step carefully out of the bath, feeling more ungainly than ever with my legs held awkwardly apart and my head covered in soapy shampoo. I looked back into the water, just for a moment, gripping the edge of the bath tightly. I swallowed back a hard lump in my throat. It looked like a crime scene from a gruesome thriller.

What do I do?

Arms shaking, I reached for my phone from the side of the sink and dialled Michael at work. I tried to speak calmly – he had been the more anxious parent-to-be throughout the pregnancy. He was at lunch, of course, because it was *midi*.

'I'm bleeding. I don't know what to do. There's lots of blood. But I feel okay.'

He replied so steadily and calmly, I could tell he was terrified. His daily default was overreaction. If I ran through from another room to find out what he was screaming and swearing about, it would be someone scoring against Man U, or the internet taking a microsecond too long to load a page.

Today, he said, 'Okay. You need to phone Dr Acharian. Tell him what's happening. I'm coming home now.'

'I don't think...should we phone him?' Cold panic coursed through me. I couldn't think clearly. 'Did he not say to phone the maternity admissions? Or maybe I should phone an ambulance? There's a lot of blood.' Even as I spoke, I had the idea in the back of my mind that the blood dispersing through the bath water might not be as much as it looked. But it was still horrifying to look at.

'Okay,' he said, 'do that then. I'm coming home.'

I hung up, then after the briefest mental rehearsal of what to say in French to the responder, dialled 112. Thank goodness, I thought, that I don't have to worry about asking for someone who can speak English.

'I'm eight months pregnant,' I quickly explained, 'and I'm bleeding heavily. My doctor is Dr Acharian at the Polyclinique de Navarre. I don't know what to do. I just started bleeding.'

The operator asked me to repeat the problem.

'I'm bleeding a lot. I don't know if I should come in.'

'Okay,' he said slowly. 'Where are you bleeding from?'

'Oh. Well, between my legs.'

'Are you injured?'

'No, nothing's happened to me. But...I'm bleeding from my uterus.'

'I see,' said the operator. 'Are you sure you need help?'

I frowned, unable to think straight, and stuttered out, 'Well...I think so.' I couldn't understand his hesitation. The intense sense of entitlement that had surprised me since early in the pregnancy, the overwhelming feeling that my special status of pregnant should bring everyone running to help, to protect my vulnerable baby, was stronger than ever. Why didn't he understand the urgency? Still, the fear of getting things wrong, of not wanting to sound stupid, fuelled my indecision again. 'Should I call my doctor instead?'

The penny dropped with what he said next.

'Madame, ce n'est pas vos règles?'

He thought I was having my period.

He thought I was a stupid foreign woman calling the emergency services on my menstruation.

I was furious at his condescension, but I swallowed my pride and repeated the important fact I had said so quickly at the start of the call, too quickly, it seemed, for him to have adjusted to my accent.

'Je suis enceinte!! J'ai huit mois!'

Now the penny dropped for him. 'Aaah, je vois! Are you alone?'

I explained Michael was on his way. Once the operator established the details, and how close Michael was, he said that Michael should drive me to the clinic, and that he would call ahead so the doctor knew we were coming.

I leaned into the bath and pulled out the plug, to spare Michael the sight of a literal bloodbath before the birth of his first child. I pushed to the back of mind the thought of any other outcome. I was still bleeding on to the floor though, with steady drips. I walked myself into the next room, our new nursery, and pulled one of the maternity pads from the hospital bag, which I had only packed the day before, after weeks of Michael's nagging to do it sooner. These pads were supposed to be used after birth, if needed, and I hadn't wanted to think about it, when we bought them: what kind of fluids they would deal with, what the aftermath of labour would be for my body.

I dressed gingerly, and was leaning over the bath trying to rinse the shampoo out of my hair when Michael arrived. Now I could see, for sure, how scared he was – I'd never seen him so drawn, but so calm. He spoke slowly and carefully, measuring his words. He picked up the hospital bag and led me out to the lift. The door slid open. Inside, he fumbled and dropped the car key. It landed right on the edge of the gap between the elevator cabin and the floor. Time slowed as the doors started closing. I held out my arm to keep them open, every muscle tensed. I couldn't think where the spare car key was.

Michael said, 'Oops.'

Not motherfucking-piece-of-shit car key. Or Jesus Christ, fuck me! Just, 'Oops.'

Then he carefully bent down and reached for the key, as if any sudden movement might send it tumbling down the lift shaft. It was caught in the gap. He tugged gently. It came loose. He put it in his pocket.

'That was lucky! Off we go then.' His face was drained of colour.

At the clinic, we were led into a treatment room where I lay on the bed. Dr Acharian arrived while the nurse fetched a monitor. 'Well,' he asked in French. 'What's happening here?'

'J'étais dans le bain, et...' I hesitated, trying to remember the expression for 'suddenly'. Michael's calm composure dropped.

'Bloody hell! Speak English!'

He was right; now was not the time for language practice. We had chosen this doctor because he was recommended by all our British expat friends – because he spoke fluent English.

I gave in. An actual medical emergency was a good enough reason for me to drop my pride and speak English to our fluent, and extremely well-paid, obstetrician. I took the pressure off and explained what had happened in English.

Moments later, a nurse attached a monitor to my belly, and to a roomful of audible sighs of relief, we heard our son's heartbeat loud and clear. Then there was an emergency C-section, and by the time Cameron was born, and Michael texted our friends with the news, Laurie replied, 'But you were just in the canteen!' Between the time when I sat up in the bath, and the birth of our son, less than ninety minutes had passed. The drama and panic of his arrival gave way to relief and morphine-fuelled elation.

Following the birth, we enjoyed a full week of care and support in the clinic, in a private room, fully covered by our insurance. This also included a short stay for Cameron in the neonatal ward – a precaution that briefly added more drama to this bilingual birth story.

It took a few days for our family members to arrive, but in the meantime we had our Pau family around us. Hannah was the first of our friends to hold Cameron, and Ben fit in a quick visit before flying off to join Mel in Canada for their wedding, when they would become Mr and Mrs Kampala.

Of course, not all the clinic and hospital staff were English speakers, so by the time we checked out I'd had a crash course in all the French vocabulary for hospitals, childbirth, maternity, and baby care.

But the language of parenthood – I was so far from fluent in that. Like any language, I could only truly learn it by doing it, by speaking it, by immersing myself and getting things wrong. It was a double immersion in a foreign culture, away from family and without the certainty of knowing where our children would grow up. Sometimes it felt too immersive, like having to gasp for breath. And the culture shock of parenthood was going to hit harder still down the line.

THE COLOURFUL RUG

Eventually, the shag rug had to go. It took nearly two years and a baby-proofing session to make me see that some modification to our French nest would be essential.

It had taken a while for the realisation to hit home: we'd been treating our home like a holiday rental. My heart sank when I thought about the ways I could have made a home a nest, where we felt we truly belonged. But by then, halfway through our stay, the idea of investing in the space with maybe only a year left felt even less worthwhile.

But when it came to that rug, I couldn't bear the thought of what a crawling little boy would discover in the depths of the ropey shag, and how quickly his discoveries would end up in his mouth. Not to mention how he would pull and tug at the stray strands until the thing would fall apart anyway.

So we rolled it up and tucked it away in a cupboard, to be discovered by future tenants. We went shopping, and in a large cardboard bin at the end of an aisle of Castorama, we found its replacement.

It was a medium-sized low pile rug with a pattern of multi-coloured squares. Its graphic style grabbed my attention: anything with stripes or squares in expertly coordinated colours easily draws my eye. The various shades of green, blue, red and orange squares, almost pixel-like, were more brightly coloured than I would normally have chosen for a grown-up living space, but the rug was cheerful and child-friendly without being childish. It was perfect, considering that our grown-up living space in our urban French apartment was about to become a playroom. Anyway, we didn't have to *love* it, because we wouldn't have it for long. There were no stray strands to get in the way of crawling and playing, and it was inexpensive, just right for a piece of temporary furnishing. We took home our new rug/play mat.

That purchase didn't go to waste. I was learning that even temporary fixtures, whether they stayed behind or came with us in the end, became part of our enduring story. I was learning to ditch that temporary mindset, once I realised that no matter how short a time we spend somewhere, the investment in our lives there and then, at that moment, was always worthwhile, whether it was about the lighting that will make a corner feel more cosy, just the right storage setup for finding flow in the kitchen, or creating a space for the pastime that gives us a moment of escape.

We have countless photos of Cameron's first year with him on that rug: lying on a baby gym and gazing up at the toys dangling above him, crawling across it with a chunky wheeled vehicle in his hand, or sitting upright delightedly banging the toy drum that was a first birthday present.

And we did take it with us, in the end.

The Playgroup

The first few weeks of new parenthood were a tsunami of overwhelming demands on my time and my body. After Cameron's dramatic birth and brief hospital stay, breast-feeding was a challenge we never quite overcame. But for the first few weeks, I spent hours alternating between failed latching attempts and pumping, until it was clear that we had to move on – I had to find a way to leave the house.

Before Cameron was born, my social life in Pau was filled with nights out and parties with those friends we had made in our first few weeks. They were Michael's colleagues, mostly, but they were *our* friends. And that continued for us as parents too – instead, we would take turns. Sometimes I got invitations to socialise with 'the other wives'. Except those weren't nights out, they were nights in, and frankly I wasn't the type of person who socialised with 'wives' or 'mums' because I had no interest in being described as a 'wife' or 'mum', thank you very much.

But I needed connection during the day, and, I had to admit, connection with people who understood what had happened to my days.

I learned that the anglophone society comprised more than the middle-aged lifers and retirees that we had met at that early barbecue. Its other main demographic was young parents, who met at a weekly playgroup. So, reluctantly, I joined them.

I got in touch with Aurélie, who was coordinating the group. In her emails, written in impeccable English, she radiated nothing but utter confidence and put-togetherness.

The first time I went was also someone's last time – bunting was up and cupcakes were on offer for a leaving party. The host welcomed me and introduced me to someone as I awkwardly laid the car seat in a corner and lifted Cameron out. An assured young British mum held the room's attention for a moment and said a few words of well wishes to the leaver, Natalie.

Although I had met a couple of the other mums in the group, that morning I knew no one in the room. But, as expats do, gradually other women saw my newness and awkwardness and spoke to me. To one friendly woman with a French accent, I said, 'You must be Aurélie?' If I had found the woman who had emailed me so reassuringly and efficiently, I had the feeling everything would be okay.

'Ah, no, I'm Christine. Aurélie is...' she looked around. 'Oh, she must be in the kitchen or something.'

As I worked my way round the room, establishing that each French woman I spoke to was not, in fact, Aurélie, I felt at sea, drifting without a glimpse of solid land. I had to find the person who had known I was coming, who was in charge, who knew something about me already. All the other accents in the room were decidedly international – mostly North American or British. Finally, I asked someone again, 'Sorry, which one is Aurélie?'

'Oh, that's her over there.' Aurélie was back in the room. And she wasn't French at all; she was the confident British woman who had spoken at the start. I approached her with double relief. Everything really was going to be okay.

'You're Catriona! You're here! Fantastic, I was worried I had scared you off!'

I told her I'd been asking all the French women in the room if they were her. 'It hadn't occurred to me that someone with that name could be anything other than French!'

'Actually, I am French,' she replied, sounding like the head girl from a school in an Enid Blyton book. 'But my mum was an international school teacher, so I sound like this. Gosh, not to worry. Easy mistake to make! Have you met everyone?' As she took my new social life in hand, guiding me into my new milieu, I was already fascinated to know more of the story of this charismatic woman, who was clearly, captivatingly, not 'just' a mum.

Over the following Thursday mornings I got to know my new tribe, and in just a few short weeks, the group I'd thought would have nothing more to offer than somewhere to be became the focal point of my week, the touchstone, a grounding source of support and connection that I couldn't imagine being without.

***

A few months later, Michael and I were side by side in bed in the early morning light, both wide awake, staring at the ceiling, holding hands. We'd been like that for an hour or more, since an early morning phone call had brought the news that his mother had died after a long illness. There wasn't much to say.

Finally, he pulled himself to a sitting position. 'I'd better get going.' He had already planned to travel back to Scotland that day, to visit his mum and spend time with her. His case was already packed, the flight booked, but the nature of the journey had changed. 'She might have waited a few hours,' he'd said, his voice thickly hollow, when he came off the call that confirmed she hadn't made it through the night.

I offered to come with him, but there was a baby to pack for, and we agreed I would catch a flight in the next couple of days, once the funeral was arranged. That sunken morning, after only fitful sleep, I was alone in the apartment with Cameron, aimless and empty, not sure what I should be feeling. Should I stay home, in mourning? Should I be looking up flights, preparing to pack? But it was Thursday morning, so I took Cameron in his baby seat down in the lift to the car. Whatever my grief should be, it was too enclosed in that little apartment in a foreign town. I needed my connection fix, the touchstone of normality, and to connect our grief to other people. It was Aurélie's turn to host, so under autumn sunshine I drove the country roads in the Pyrenean foothills to her house.

On the drive, I reminded myself to be honest. I imagined myself answering that ordinary greeting, 'How are you?' with a reflexive, cheery 'Fine!' then having to say, 'Well, actually...' with an awkward, apologetic non-laugh, and deliver the worst kind of news. Or worse, that I might give my automatic answer, and the conversation would move on, or continue from before I walked in, then I would spend the rest of the time wondering how to get it in the conversation, without disturbing the mood. Or, worst of all, that I would tell no one, and my feelings, my non-feelings, my help-me-know-how-to-feel feelings, would stay secret, and would I feel separate and dissociated, the opposite of what I needed. How British of me, spending half an hour figuring out the most polite way to convey a death in the family.

In the end, as the others were greeting me, I just blurted it out. 'My mother-in-law died last night.' I reddened at the thought of demanding their attention and sympathy. But I knew they wouldn't want me to be anything other than honest. We were there for each other, not for small talk and comparing baking.

We probably stayed for lunch that day. Because Aurélie lived about half an hour out of town, she always offered lunch as an enticement, and it felt like being looked after, as she efficiently bustled in her cluttered kitchen putting together some easy-yet-healthy pasta for the kids.

That day, I didn't want to be anywhere else than among my new tribe of 'mums', where each person was an articulate, funny, clever, unique woman. Each had talents, qualifications, skills, and interests. Some had had a successful career, others were running businesses. Some were looking for work; some were making the most of the opportunity to be a full-time parent, while others resented the obligation. Some had lived in many countries already, others were feeling utterly foreign and desperately missing home. We were a town planner, a designer, teachers, an HR exec, an orthodontist. It just so happened that we'd all had a baby in the last three years (when children start school in France) and that we needed a connection. The babies fed and slept, and the toddlers played with other children's toys, while the adults talked, offloaded, connected, and got to know each other, providing a point of contact in the week, where we had common experiences, and so much to learn from each other.

The first lesson I learned was not to judge a group by its label – to let go of some internalised misogyny and not to assume I knew them before I met them.

Then, I learned how to connect quickly, to welcome every new connection as a potential part of our family of proximity, the people we would reach out to in the worst of times.

They were our last-minute emergency babysitters, and our emergency contact people, and our friends. We might have to rely on each other within weeks of meeting.

Each conversation with someone new in my life in France would start with, 'Where are you from?' Then there would be a barrage of questions, back and forth, until we knew each other's stories: *Why are you here? How long have you been here? Where else have you lived? How long will you stay? Have you found a doctor, a dentist? Do you need help with visa paperwork, getting the internet connected?*

Friendship happened in a hurry.

THE TEST

Cameron's first birthday was on a Thursday, so that morning I hosted playgroup for a teddy bear's picnic first birthday party in our apartment. The sofa was once more pushed back against the balcony window to make space for about a dozen mums and their under-threes. Birthday boy Cameron discovered chocolate cake for the first time and made the most of it.

My parents were visiting, both to celebrate and to help me out, since Michael had to go on a three-week work trip to Nigeria. Once all the playgroup mums had herded their little ones out the door and down in the lift, my mum helped me clear up, and we wiped the chocolate frosting from Cameron's face. My dad came back from his morning café visit with his crossword, just in time to miss the worst of the chaos.

That morning, I couldn't ignore the possibility that there might be another cause for celebration. But I kept the thought to myself. As I got dressed I'd been thinking, *hmm, my boobs don't normally get this sore before my period*. Then, *it's lasting a few days longer this time*. And then, eventually, in slow motion, my brain caught up.

It was crystal clear why I had been getting so tired the last few days.

Michael and I had agreed we would start trying for a second child after a year – yet here I was on Cameron's first birthday, wondering when I could find out discreetly whether I was already pregnant. For the next two days, I did my best to slip out nonchalantly and pick up a pregnancy test.

But it was impossible; either my parents and I already had plans, or one of them would pop out with me to get something they had forgotten to pack, or to keep me company. There was no way I was going to reveal my suspicions to anyone before I could tell Michael, so I just had to be cool, and wait.

By the Friday evening, with plans to meet friends at our favourite Mexican restaurant for dinner, I was desperately hoping for a chance to be sure – because if I wasn't pregnant, I could enjoy a few beers. On the way into town, I checked all the little grocery shops, willing French regulations to have changed overnight so they could sell tests at the checkout as in other countries. But no, I would have to wait till my next opportunity to visit a pharmacy.

I needn't have worried I was missing out though – I could barely stay awake for dessert, never mind after knocking back a few beers.

Finally, over the weekend, I got out for a solo walk. Back home, I snuck back into that tiny toilet cupboard and confirmed the obvious: I was indeed already pregnant.

I saved the information and the test as a surprise for Michael's return from Nigeria, with my mum deeply concerned by my sudden afternoon napping habit, suggesting maybe I should get checked for anaemia. 'Don't worry mum, it's just a heavy period,' I mumbled from my stupor on the sofa. She later said that she couldn't believe she missed it.

Of course, Michael was delighted with his surprise welcome home present. But there was a problem.

***

We were nearing the end of our three years in Pau, of our 'temporary' time away. It had been clear for long enough now that despite all my talk of a three-year career break, and a temporary stay, and despite the Denby plates in the attic in Aberdeen, we would make an onward move after Pau, not a return move. The career opportunities for anyone willing to be globally mobile were far richer and more varied than anything on offer back home for Michael. Having spent two and half years immersed in the international community that centred around the company's Pau HQ, hearing stories from families who had lived on every continent, for whom it was a normal expectation, a natural progression,

I had settled into that expectation myself, that I would make another move to somewhere different.

Maybe I wasn't getting to move 'home' this time, but moving on would mean a chance to start afresh, to get away from the frustrations of life in France. With the knowledge of our imminent departure, it was even easier to frame the irritations of daily culture shock as 'not normal', and something I'd be away from soon.

Nigeria came up first. Michael had already lived there on rotation. Angola was mentioned too. Any nerves I had at the thought of living in these distant, unknown places were eased by the time I'd spent in our international community, and conversations with people, like Eve, who'd already lived there, for whom life had continued, raising children, making friends, until the strange became normal.

Eventually, Michael came home one day early in March and told me there was an interesting job in Brazil, and that he might be considered for it. But, he said, 'don't start planning a life there or anything! Nothing's decided yet. It's just a possibility.'

I knew his company made a lot of these decisions at the last minute. Still, I couldn't help imagining my new life...caipirinhas and salsa, exploring South America, learning the gorgeous Portuguese language...

At that time, it was fairly likely that Ben and Mel were on track to move to Angola, so Mel and I decided that we would learn Portuguese together in the final months of our time in Pau. I resolved I would definitely have to hire a personal trainer, to get my post-C-section body ready for the Brazilian beaches.

And then, a couple of weeks later, we weren't going to Brazil.

Out of the blue, Michael said, 'How about Uganda?'

This was not a destination I'd ever heard other expats talking about. I pressed pause on my inner montage of life in Rio.

The company hadn't been working in Uganda for long, so Michael got in touch with some colleagues currently working there. 'They say it's a good place to live – they're enjoying themselves. There are lots of international schools. It's safe, and Kampala is a busy cosmopolitan city.'

I prepared myself for the idea of moving there. With Michael's experience of living in Nigeria, in a location where daily life had been precarious and not family-friendly, I trusted his instinct that it could be a good move for us. The idea of living on the African continent definitely held a thrill, and Uganda was mostly English-speaking, so that would make things easier.

Not everyone was so easily reassured. I waited until we were sure the move was happening before I said 'Uganda' on the phone to my mum. My parents were supportive, and reassured by Michael's experience of life on the continent (he'd lived in Nigeria and Egypt in his childhood too), but the absolute foreignness, to them, of the idea worried them.

I said to my mum, 'Of course, you can come and visit.' They had travelled to Pau several times. 'Just think – you'll be able to go on safari!'

'Oh.' The thought had never even occurred to her until that moment. 'Oh. Well. Maybe. We'll see.'

I was grateful, though, that my family supported us, even if they harboured secret doubts. I had friends whose family 'back home' openly expressed negative opinions about moving abroad, and the choice of destination.

I prepared myself for the idea of moving to Uganda. I struggled to create a visual of my potential life there, one that didn't stem from eighties news reports or colonial historical cinema. But I knew that there was a lot more to it than that. Most tempting was the knowledge that we would soon go on safari, something I had always imagined would be a once-in-a-lifetime, once-I'm-retired kind of holiday.

It was certainly to be an adventure, albeit one I was pretty uncertain about. But we would be on the adventure together.

Then came news that heightened my anticipation.

I stood in the kitchen stirring a pot, with Cameron gurgling in the high chair behind me, as I watched Michael take off his jacket and disappear into the bedroom to change from his work clothes.

'So I have news,' came the muffled shout through the apartment.

Then he was leaning against the kitchen door-frame. 'Guess where the Kampalas are going next?' He had a twinkle in his eye that made me gasp and widen my eyes.

'Um...' did I dare say it? 'Uganda?'

'Yes! Ben's been offered a job there, too.'

'So definitely not Angola? We're *all* going to Uganda?'

'Yep.'

We had struck expat gold. To go on a new adventure, with all the fresh opportunities and new friendships ahead, was one thing. But to arrive with close friends beside us, the family we had chosen, beside us to share the adventure? This was going to be a hundred times better.

***

Now, everything changed.

We had barely set our Uganda plans in motion before Michael had to visit Nigeria. Travelling to Uganda required a yellow fever vaccine – we wouldn't get in the country without it. It was a live vaccine that wasn't recommended during pregnancy, unless completely necessary.

And now I was pregnant. We'd missed the window.

The situation felt impossible. He had a job there, and I couldn't go. I couldn't stay in France, not in our current situation anyway, with the company paying our rent. We didn't have a home of our own to go back to in Scotland – both our flats were rented out. Could we ask our tenants to leave, so that I could move back in? That didn't feel fair; it probably went against our lease terms. Anyway – whether in Aberdeen or Pau, me living on my own with a toddler and a pregnancy wasn't ideal. I couldn't imagine moving in with my parents for nine months. By now, Aberdeen was the place I called home, and they were three hours away on the Clyde coast.

But we had to agree that Michael would start the job in Uganda, and somehow, I would move back to Scotland until after the baby was born, when I could get vaccinated and join him. The company agreed to give him a status that would let him travel back and forward more often. It would work out eventually.

But we had screwed up the timing.

All the excitement and anticipation I'd felt the day that Michael told me that Ben and Mel were going with us, and then again, when he came home from Nigeria and I shared our exciting news, fell away. I couldn't look forward any more – the adventure was out of reach, and I already felt isolated. My life was beyond my control.

I tried to explain the overwhelming frustration to Michael: 'I'm not in control of my body, because the pregnancy and breast-feeding are taking charge of that. I'm not in control of my time, because that belongs to a toddler. I'm not in control of my future, because that's up to the company.'

'Oh, come on,' he said, 'things aren't that bad, your life isn't out of control.'

'No, it's not *out* of control, that's not what I said.' I brushed away frustrated tears. 'I said it's not in *my* control.'

THE LEAVING PRESENTS

O n a hot June day, we gathered under the sun with all our friends, in the small garden in front of Hannah's house, for our leaving party. There was barbecuing, and breads and salads emerging from Hannah's tiny kitchen out on to the deck, and a lot of beers and glasses of champagne and rosé and I'm sure, given the Canadian contingent, someone was making caesars. Someone always turned up with the ingredients for making the Canadians' favourite vodka-tomato juice cocktail.

As the afternoon drifted into the balmy evening, we put one-year-old Cameron down in Hannah's spare bedroom, hoping he would sleep enough that we could stay a while longer. Later, on my way inside to check on him, I paused in the lounge for a chat with one of our American friends, another friend crush of mine. I looked up to her because she was clever and intense and always interested and sincere – no emotion left unspoken. 'But how are you feeling?' she asked, her clear eyes searching mine. 'I mean, really?'

'Well,' I must have said, ever-reasonable, ever balancing the challenges with the privilege, 'it's not ideal, but I'm looking forward to being back for a while. And it's not for too long. Then I'll join the others, and we'll all get to hang out again.'

'Honestly,' she said, 'I just think you're amazing. What you're doing is going to be so difficult, such a challenge. For you and Michael to be apart, and you'll be just you and the baby, and another one on the way...such a tough decision you've made. I'm just in complete awe of you. You're a strong mama, you're going to have a beautiful family. I just admire you so much.'

As we hugged, I blinked back hot tears. I was grateful to retreat to the darkened hush in the spare bedroom, our firstborn snuffling in his pop-up cot. Pregnant, overwhelmed, and stone cold sober, I took a few minutes to let the tears flow despite the muffled party chatter. But they weren't tears of goodbye grief.

My American friend wasn't the first to have said something similar to me, and she was absolutely sincere in her compliments. But I felt hotly resentful. Why couldn't people understand that the last thing I wanted to hear was how difficult my life was about to become? I was hormonal and vulnerable, and lacking the party buzz that everyone else was imbibing. Why did everyone want to talk about that one thing with me, instead of just letting me celebrate?

A few deep breaths and the moment passed. It was up to me to celebrate, and I was determined to keep going as long as possible. Michael the pessimist was convinced that Cameron would not sleep for long through the party, but we had trained him well, through travel and dinner parties and busy Burns Suppers. I was sure he would sleep a good bit longer so I could enjoy these last special times with our friends.

Back among the celebrations, presents were being exchanged. Hannah had organised and framed thoughtful photo collages of festivals, group hikes, picnics and parties. I unwrapped a selection of cookbooks with local Béarnaise and Basque recipes. Ben and Mel were handing out fridge magnets to everyone with their faces on, determined that no one would forget them. They were wearing the T-shirts that Michael and I had given them, making a joke out of the fact that they shared their family name with the city we were all moving to: 'Yes, my name really is Kampala.'

Except I wasn't going with them. Not yet anyway.

It was hard to celebrate with everyone else at our leaving party: Ben and Mel with their T-shirts, Michael off to join them, to kick off this adventure with them in a new city, while I was leaving for months of solo parenting and Scottish weather.

I did my best to enjoy myself, willing the circumstances to let me pretend for a while. But ultimately Cameron wouldn't settle. Michael was annoyed. 'I told you he wouldn't be able to sleep here! We should have taken turns to come to the party.'

I fought back hot tears, frustrated that he couldn't see that it was worth the effort for us both to be here and have fun together with our friends – even more frustrated that he'd been right.

I took Cameron home while Michael enjoyed the rest of the party.

But among the tears and resentment, there was truth in what I had said to our American friend. I *was* looking forward to going home. I was going back to that pin on the map, back to a place I knew, where things were *normal*. I would have a break from the differentness and the unfamiliar. Despite the upheaval of separating the family, of pregnancy and a new baby, I could feel normal again, because I would be back where I belonged. I'd see friends every weekend, watch films in actual VO, and go to shops where everything was under one roof, on exactly the right shelf. My time in Scotland would let me feel rooted again, would give me a holiday from being foreign. I would have solid ground under my feet, and feel refreshed and prepared for the next foreign place.

I'd feel at home again, surely.

PART TWO: SOMEONE ELSE'S HOUSE, ABERDEENSHIRE

THE UNEMPTIED DRAWERS

Once, when we were dating, Michael absentmindedly referred to the 'grounds' of his family's house.

'Excuse me...grounds?' I raised my eyebrows at him. 'Your house has grounds?'

'Oh, no no no!' He tried to grab back the words. 'It's just a garden. Like, it's a big garden. But no, we don't have grounds, it's not like a country estate or anything!'

And he was right. But it was a big garden. The house sat in the middle of its plot of land, with green space all around it, and a wide driveway leading from the road. Michael's parents moved into it when he was already an adult, although he moved in briefly, when he was between flats.

It was a grand-looking house of imposing red sandstone and multiple gables, its architecture suggesting more than the actual number of rooms. It stood out at one end of the village, bordered by fields on two sides, and with a ten-metre tall tree visible from well outside the village.

It made perfect sense, on paper, or in our reasonable planning full of rational suggestions, for Cameron and I to move in there while Michael got on with his new job in Uganda. The year before, my mother-in-law had passed away after struggling with illness. My father-in-law was alone in the big house. With my sister-in-law and her toddler, just a few months older than Cameron, along the road at the other end of the village, there would be family support around me, and space enough for me to settle in without having to bother my father-in-law too much. I would take regular trips back and forward to my own parents, two-and-a-half hours' drive away. The house I grew up in was big enough for a family, but big enough to house an adult with her own family, in the company of eager grandparents? A bit tight for that, not every day for ten months, anyway.

I arrived back in Scotland in August 2012, four months before baby number two was due. We understood that the yellow fever vaccination could be given from six months onwards, so expected that I would be there for ten months, until the baby would be old enough for his own jab.

Michael came with me to get us settled in. I stepped into the en-suite guest room, the cosiest of the bedrooms, and the one with its own large, airy bathroom, giving plenty of space for baby bathing and supplies.

The room had two twin beds side by side, separated by a dresser. When we had visited, Michael and I would sometimes push the beds together, sometimes put up with it for the sake of a day or two.

I quickly assessed the layout, this time as a resident, not a guest. My gaze darted around the furniture, mentally repositioning things in the way that would work best. It was exactly what I had done when I first arrived at university, in a room in halls which looked exactly the same as every other room, same furniture, same layout.

'Okay,' I said to Michael, 'before you go you'll have to help me move the beds together, on the other wall.'

'Maybe we should check with my dad first?' he said. 'Why do you need to move them, anyway?'

'I need to make this room work for me over the next few months. Having the beds separated takes up too much room. I'll need to get a cot in here, and if the beds are on that wall I can set this up as a nursing corner. See? With the TV right opposite. Then I don't have to sit in bed to watch TV.' I looked around, then turned back to Michael. 'Anyway, it doesn't make any difference to your dad where the furniture is, does it? While I'm using the room? I hope he knows what he's let himself in for.'

From the beginning, I was pretty sure he didn't. He was absolutely generous from the start – more than happy to accept our suggestion of having me and a boy and a bump in his home, but I don't think he quite understood how disruptive our presence would become to his routine middle-aged life. Having us live there – bringing our possessions, our toys, cooking our own food, coming and going – was different from us stopping for a visit and living out of suitcases for a couple of weeks. I'm not sure he saw that until we were well and truly installed.

After a couple of days of catching up with the family, and with the beds in their new position, I set about unpacking, mentally and logistically preparing myself for the months ahead in this space, keen to feel at home and nested, but conscious of not wanting to overstep the boundaries of the space that it would be reasonable for us to take up. In my own parents' house, I would feel like it was my domain, but here, I was keen to please, to be a good guest. In fact, I thought, that was a positive thing: an adult daughter treating her parents' home like she would have as a teenager would not have been the healthiest backdrop to becoming a parent of two.

I opened the first couple of drawers in a low dresser, the empty ones we would usually use for bits and pieces when we came for visits. Then I opened the drawers below. They were all full, with linens and spare towels. Another tall dresser in the corner held spare knits, tablecloths, and drawers full of old relics from Michael's and his sister's youth.

The drawers under the beds were full of blankets and more spare bedding.

I needed a strategy here. I couldn't just dump all these things out of the drawers to make space for myself. I went out on to the landing, where another large dresser stood, crossing my fingers. Every drawer was brimming with more spare bedding and chunky knits.

Luckily, Michael was still around.

'You'll have to explain to your dad that he needs to find somewhere for those things in all the drawers. I need space to unpack.'

My father-in-law took the news stoically. 'Oh, aye, well, right enough.' He hadn't thought of that. 'I don't know where I'm going to keep it all, mind you.'

Every fibre of my being wanted to get elbow deep in decluttering on his behalf. Quite apart from the unworn clothes, there were unopened bedding sets, bought in sales but never used, and soft furnishings brought from previous houses. And how many chunky knit jumpers did a person need, even in the north-east of Scotland?

But none of that was for me to get involved in. My place was in the guest room, and the guest bathroom, and later, it would be in a corner of the lounge where we set up a play area with Cameron's toys.

My father-in-law set about finding new places to store the contents of the guest room drawers. 'I just don't know where I'm going to put it all though, there isn't anywhere else.' I bit my tongue, and he found the space.

He even emptied the drawer in the guest bathroom, which I had marvelled at for years, with its collection of dozens of compact and stylish wash bags from business class travel, all kept, just in case.

Then, our shipment arrived.

This was probably the moment when my father-in-law realised the extent of what he had agreed to. We had divided the shipment as we left France, so that a few things went to Scotland while the rest went to Uganda. It had not been fun, heavily pregnant, at the height of southern French summer with no air conditioning, to categorise our possessions as 'here', 'there', and 'somewhere else'. Inevitably, there were mistakes, and the reclining chair we had bought in France as a nursing chair for Cameron arrived here instead of Uganda. Michael was attached to it, but I couldn't believe we had kept that cheap velour breast-milk-stained thing, stained also with the tears of the heart-breaking weeks when we tried and failed at breast-feeding. It got carted upstairs along with boxes of baby equipment and clothes.

Our toys arrived too, and I bought a small cube storage system for the corner of the lounge. We had kept the colourful rug we bought in France, our first proper investment in our home there, and I laid it as a play rug in front of the toys, delineating a small corner where we could contain our clutter. These were the spaces we took up, me and a boy and a baby-to-be, apart from a changing mat in the downstairs loo, a high chair in the dining room, and some plastic sippy cups in the corner of a kitchen cupboard.

No one but me imposed any limits on the space we took up, yet I couldn't help feeling that we filled up too much of it.

But at least I was back home, in the land where I belonged.

THE HAND-PAINTED PLATE

With Michael settling in to life in Uganda, I started to find a routine in the small community. It was my third time pushing a toddler and heaving my bump along to the other end of the village. The playgroup took place every Wednesday morning in a large communal room sandwiched between the primary school and the small room that served as a part-time library.

I turned the corner at the village hotel, walked past the village shop in the village square, and along the road that led to a whisky distillery. When I reached the school, I crossed the playground, parked the buggy under a shelter, and joined the other mums, occasional dads, babies and toddlers.

I knocked on the solid, heavy door to be let in, since it was carefully locked to make sure no toddlers could inadvertently stray into the big unsafe outside.

Inside, storage cupboards lined the room, each labelled for use by various community groups. There was a piano on one side, and kitchen units with kettle and utilitarian tea things in the opposite corner. The volunteers who arrived first had set up the kids' favourite toys in different play areas, as well as play mats with hanging distractions for babies to lie on while their mums chatted.

I wasn't aware how much I was expecting from my third appearance until it didn't happen. I entered the room and looked around, smiling – beaming – expectantly. No one looked my way.

'Morning!' I sang out, and one lady near the door murmured, 'Hi there,' before returning to her toddler's sippy cup. My sister-in-law was yet to arrive that morning, so I didn't have the usual crutch of the person I already knew to target and start a conversation with.

I settled Cameron with some kind of wheeled playthings, and settled myself and the bump carefully on one of the chairs set against the edges of the room to watch him, aware that I still had a smile self-consciously plastered on my face.

***

What had I been expecting? What was it that didn't happen?

I wanted to be like Norm, in that bar in Boston where everybody knows your name.

I had walked into that playgroup after just two previous visits, expecting everyone to turn their smiles my way and declare 'Catriona's here!' After just two visits, I expected everyone to know my name, to pull me into their conversations, to ask me all about how my day, my week, my month was going.

They didn't.

Was I being unreasonable?

After a few minutes, I relaxed and made my way to the corner with the comforting low rumble of the urn and the tinkle of spoons in teacups, and gladly accepted a cup of tea from a volunteer. I turned to someone I'd met the week before and seized on the recognition I spied in her eye contact. 'How has your week been?' I said.

She met my direct question with a warm and friendly response. But there were other conversations going on around me, between women who had known each other for years – or even decades. Many of these mums were lifelong friends; they'd known each other since primary school. Others, like my sister-in-law, were recent arrivals into the newly built houses at the edge of the village, but were settling in for the long term, planning for the secondary school these children would all be attending together ten years from now.

Others lived out of the village in the country, where they were slowly renovating an old house for their family's future, or where they were the third or fourth generation farming the land.

And yet, after only two weeks, I thought I could walk into a roomful of new friends? As an absolute stranger to almost all the people there? My imagined

Cheers moment was an impossible idea. What kind of weirdo expects that sense of belonging after two short weeks?

An expat, that's who. Even one who's only been away for three years.

On the walk back through the village, pushing the toddler and heaving the bump, I realised that for the first couple of weeks I had gone into that playgroup exactly as I had done with my playgroup in Pau. I'd forgotten that my definition of 'normal' had already shifted.

I'd sat down next to strangers and bombarded them with personal questions, eager to tell them my story in return. But I was a strange new person in the village – an over-confident one at that. Why should my story be especially interesting to them? They would get to know me in their own time, in the normal way.

Which they did, to be fair. Several months later, I definitely had a new group of friends – we'd been out for dinner together, and when it was time for me to leave again, someone organised a send-off for me at a ceramic painting cafe. They surprised me afterwards with a plate that everyone in the playgroup had painted a message on. That hand-painted plate has hung in each of our homes ever since.

But it was a surprise that, in just three years abroad, I had changed too much to go back to the way things were. There would be no slotting back into my old life, or even 'old life with added babies'. In fact, perhaps I even felt more at home among people whose own sense of home was fluid and transient. I had a new perspective on life, on people, on myself, one that meant going 'home' had become something else entirely – even though I didn't know what that something else was, not yet.

THE GETAWAY CAR

One Thursday in November, nearly eight months pregnant, I loaded Cameron into his car seat and heaved myself and my enormous bump into the driving seat. The Golf I was driving, inherited from Michael's mum, was proving a bit more spacious in its driving position than our previous car in France. During my first pregnancy, I'd had to stop driving earlier, as the steering wheel and the bump jostled for the same space. Still, I wouldn't have much longer in this car either, before I would have to rely on someone else to drive me around. And in a village this size, the driving around was essential.

I drove out of the village, along country roads, until joining the busy north-south dual carriageway for a brief spell. We took the turnoff for Stonehaven, the pretty coastal market town where Michael had spent much of his childhood, and where I would drop Cameron off for his one day a week at a friendly nursery.

Driving down into Stonehaven, which nestled on the shore around a sheltered bay, was like taking refuge from the village. In the village, with each walk to the park, or to the local shop, I would inevitably bump into someone I knew, especially at the park. Or at least, someone who knew who I was, and I knew who they were, which is not the same as being known. On the weekends, I would take Cameron to play, and usually meet another family there – a mum from the playgroup, but out for a walk as the whole family, the couple watching their kids play. On some days, the fact that there was always someone to stop and say hello to somehow exacerbated my sense of solitude in the village, like a magnifying lens was focused on my solo status, just me and a stroller and a bump. From the outside, I probably looked self-sufficient and capable – the kind of person who would choose to spend this time separated from my partner, being a newcomer, managing with the minimum of help. But being recognised made my solitude feel deeply visible.

In the market town on the coast there were people everywhere, getting on with their day, day-trippers and even tourists walking along the coastal paths, and cafés to sit in where I wouldn't be recognised. It felt more normal to be alone there. On nursery days, I would often drop Cameron off, then stay in the town for the day. I could relax into the mild buzz of the small town.

But even better was the buzz of Aberdeen itself, the city I had once chosen as home. I'd thought of returning to the region as returning to the city, but the village just wasn't quite close enough – a forty-minute drive (while pregnant, with a toddler) doesn't allow for a lot of spontaneity. Making plans with my friends from 'before' required a lot of planning and didn't happen very often, and anyway, it had only taken three years for a lot of those relationships to have shifted. Meanwhile, the friends who were still close and in touch had their own family lives to get on with day to day.

There had been none of the invitations I expected to join my friends and their families for Sunday lunch, or friends letting me know they were free for a drink if I was in town. I was close, but out of sight, and out of mind. Just down the road, but not round the corner.

So it was only on nursery days I could take myself off to the city. Perhaps I'd meet a friend for lunch, but mostly I would please myself in even greater anonymity.

This was a special Thursday, and I had a big plan. I needed Cameron to settle quickly, and not be too clingy this morning, which he wasn't. I parked at Stonehaven station. I had carefully checked the train times to be sure that I would have time to get to Aberdeen, do what I wanted to do, and catch the train back in time for picking Cameron up.

This was something I hadn't done for years, and I knew it had to be today, this Thursday. I was getting closer and closer to my due date, and even today I was crossing my fingers that the little buddy inside wasn't ready for an early appearance.

A mid-week, mid-morning showing of the new James Bond film (*Skyfall*) was hardly crowded – there were maybe two other people in the cinema – as many as I might meet during a visit to the park in the village. But I was completely anonymous, and completely myself. No one else in the shopping mall multiplex cared who I was, or that I was alone, as I bought my ticket that morning. (Certainly, none of them knew that my husband and our best friends had been to the premier showing of the film in Kampala. Nor that they had dressed up for the occasion, enjoying the atmosphere of the Ugandan audience relishing a big new movie release, dressed in Bond-style tuxes and all their best Hollywood glamour, as much as the film itself.)

Dressed instead for an Aberdeen winter, carefully manoeuvring my bump along the row as I balanced my indulgent bucket of popcorn, I was in my happy place, reminding myself of the freedom of city living, of my pre-parenting days. Remembering my film classes from university, and how I wrote about James Bond as an example for my final dissertation – remembering when I was that thinking, analytical, pop-culture person. Maybe I would have loved sharing one of my very favourite things to do (to always get to the cinema for the new Bond film) with someone else, but that day, I absolutely loved being there alone.

Daniel Craig unveiled the iconic Aston Martin to Judi Dench, her getaway car, ready to whisk her north, away from danger, to the Scottish countryside. As they rolled through the hills and the heather to the Bond family's country retreat, I relaxed into the comfort of my cinema seat. For a couple of hours, I reclaimed the independence that felt like something from my core. An independence that I felt like I'd recklessly, unthinkingly surrendered.

I had escaped from my country retreat, and found myself at home in my personal city-village, surrounded by strangers; I had retreated from the countryside to myself, just for a couple of hours.

THE ACCIDENTAL CHAIR

'So, how do you feel about a C-section now?'

I stared at the calendar on the consultant obstetrician's desk in Aberdeen Maternity Hospital and took another moment to reflect. After Cameron's emergency birth, when I hadn't even gone into labour before he was born, I wondered if I had missed out on a rite of passage into motherhood. A lifetime of watching TV scenes with messy waters breaking, women screaming as they white-knuckled their partner's hand, and agony turning to ecstasy when the moment finally came, had prepared me to endure that moment myself, as terrifying as it seemed. It was hard to shake off the idea that I was missing something, although plenty of friends were more than happy to convince me I was the lucky one.

But at my previous appointment the consultant had been keen to point out the risks of following an emergency section with a natural birth, and reassured me that the recovery would be much easier from a planned surgery. My due date was very close to Christmas, and Michael was in Uganda. He'd have to travel as close as possible to the due date to be able to stay with us over the holidays.

I turned to face the consultant. 'Yes,' I said, 'let's do it. Let's get this one into the diary.' It was a relief to know we could reliably plan for Michael to be there.

But early in December, I made a panicked call to Uganda. At my pre-surgical assessment, the midwife discovered I was carrying a very fidgety baby who wouldn't stay in a birth-ready position, so, with snow on the country roads, they admitted me for monitoring, a full week ahead of the scheduled date.

I spoke to Michael at work that Friday afternoon. 'They're admitting me to hospital! You have to come home, now. Cameron needs you. Anything could happen!' My father-in-law was more than happy to step out of his usual routine to look after Cameron, but in the heat of the moment, I couldn't imagine getting through the days ahead without Michael. I was untethered; only he could hold the other end of the rope.

Michael cancelled his ticket for his company's festive party that night, and caught a flight the following day. He arrived late on Saturday night at his dad's house, and on Sunday he came along the hospital corridor with Cameron to see me. In the end, he was there only one day earlier than his originally planned arrival time.

His brow was knitted with concern, then when he saw me, his jaw dropped at the size I'd become. He was convinced this time I was even bigger than I'd been the first time around.

Otherwise, I was just fine. Truthfully, the initial panic at the idea of a hospital admission had passed, and I was enjoying my break away from parenting a toddler while heaving a bump around. I was still relieved to have our family back together on the same soil.

That week in hospital turned out to be a gift. I wasn't in any pain, other than the discomfort of an enormous belly, and I was in a quiet ward with other pre-natal mums. Friends in Aberdeen popped in to see me, I caught up on reading and TV shows, and bought myself chocolate from the hospital shop whenever I wanted.

What I gradually realised was that the most precious part of that gifted week was freedom from guilt. In that hospital bed, months of holding myself inside a self-imposed space melted away. So did months of straining not to impose my needs on others. I'd spent most of that year, since before the move, fitting myself into other people's plans, other people's routines. Because I'd felt like I was asking so much of other people, I didn't notice I had convinced myself I didn't need more, *shouldn't* ask for more. That phone call to Michael in Uganda had felt like an indulgence.

But here I was, for the good of my baby's health and my own, comfortable, sleeping alone, and with an actual buzzer by my side for the sole purpose of getting me what I needed.

Being right there in the hospital did make me wonder if I still had the 'opportunity' to go into labour before the C-section. In fact, I was positively willing my waters to break that Wednesday, when it dawned on me why that date, the one the doctor first calculated, hadn't been available. It was December 12, 2012. Could I make my second son's date of birth 12/12/12? But no, he was still fidgeting around in there. So on the Friday morning a porter rolled me along to surgery as scheduled, with no drama, no misunderstandings, no searching for words in a foreign language. Just a delivery that went as planned – except for cheeky moments-old Ben peeing on my shoulder as he was handed to Michael – then post-surgical bliss in the recovery room with a latching baby and curious toddler.

A week after we arrived back at the house in the village with Ben, he had his first Christmas, and we had our first as a family of four. A few days into the new year, before returning to Uganda, Michael drove me to my parents' house, where I would stay for another few weeks, until I could drive again – not possible for six weeks after a section.

From then until April, I shifted between the two houses, each time reestablishing myself and my little family of three, negotiating the space I felt we could take up. Rearranging a kitchen cupboard so I could put back the baby bottles. Finding a time to pump. Remembering how someone else preferred to load the dishwasher, arranging meal times, and constantly hearing myself say 'sorry' and 'thank you' no matter how much I tried to stop myself, no matter how much I reminded myself I was allowed to fill these spaces.

I remember one drive back north, arriving in the early-evening dark of a Scottish winter, when Ben had been screaming in the back for the last twenty minutes of the two-and-a-half-hour drive. I could tell why from the smell. My father-in-law was away; the house was dark and empty. I dashed from the car, keeping my hands free to deactivate the alarm. Then I dashed back to get screaming Ben from his car seat; as I lifted him, my heart sank and my stomach turned. I was dealing with an up-the-back explosion, with leakage all over his clothes and the seat. I left Cameron asleep in his car seat and carried Ben in front of me through the house to the downstairs loo, where there was a changing mat. But the changing mat had been tidied away. I lifted Ben onto my shoulder, surrendering now to the inevitable change of clothes for both of us, and one-handedly opened the cupboard to retrieve the changing mat, to re-establish our presence in the house. It was a relief to lay him down finally, get him changed and buckled into the recliner on his Tripp Trapp high chair, with his favourite floppy multicoloured monkey toy to entertain him, and return to Cameron in his car seat – thankfully still sleeping and oblivious. I got both boys inside, but our luggage would have to wait until later. I ran upstairs for a quick change of clothes, then ventured into the kitchen, exhausted and tearful, to find something for our dinner.

Living between both sets of grandparents meant there were plenty of meals I didn't have to think about, and there was help with the laundry, and clean sheets to sleep in. Still, between addresses, and between two children under two, there was no headspace to process how quickly I had become the parent of a baby and toddler, and no real nest of my own to thrive in as a new mama bird.

But it turned out I was grateful for the accidental chair – that stained velour recliner that got delivered to the village instead of Uganda.

After it arrived in the shipment and the movers carried it upstairs, I placed it in my room, in a corner behind the door, opposite the TV. I had a small bedside table beside it, then added Ben's rocking cradle on the other side of that. When I was staying in the house in the village, I would retreat to that chair in the evenings, at least until Ben was sleeping, then often I would stay there to watch TV while he snuffled beside me, rather than take the monitor downstairs and join my father-in-law in the grand but cosy lounge.

For sure, Ben cried and fussed just like every baby, but I treasure memories from the months after his birth of sitting in that chair in the light of a table lamp, with him feeding – more successfully, more peacefully than I'd ever managed with Cameron. There was a lot of coming and going that Scottish winter, moments of feeling untethered and uprooted. But nothing could have been more grounding than sharing that chair with a feeding baby. Sometimes, the more constrained a space is, the more it can feel like a nest. For a moment, at least.

THE BUSINESS CLASS FLIGHT

I wanted that intensely vulnerable time to be over as soon as possible. Just as tiny Ben relied on me and the rest of the family, I felt the dependency on everyone around me made me small and soft. And I was physically vulnerable too – recovering from two pregnancies within two years, major surgery, displaced and in constant transition for four years. Without a sense of place and togetherness, I was more rootless than ever. What happens when a body has all that to recover from?

A kind of collapse, perhaps?

The worst night of my life?

***

In the spring, Michael came back to Scotland to take his family to Uganda. It turned out we didn't have to wait as long as we'd originally thought. While we were right in thinking the yellow fever vaccine couldn't be given before six months old, Ben was allowed to travel without it, and then get vaccinated after we got there. I got the vaccine so that I could travel, meaning that I had to stop breastfeeding – those peaceful moments of 'home' were behind me.

For the first time in my life, I was completely unprepared for my arrival in a new country. I'd always revelled in the anticipation of travel, poring over guidebooks, learning the basics of a new language, studying maps.

But this time, even though I was in almost daily contact with Uganda over FaceTime, and hearing stories from Ben – we called him Big Ben now – and

Mel, as well as from Michael about their life in the bustling capital city, I had made no headspace at all to try to envisage our life there.

I knew they (we) lived in a luxury apartment complex, but I couldn't shake from my mind images of post-colonial savannah living, a disconcerting mix of period films and Live Aid footage. I knew Kampala was a big, busy city full of offices and restaurants, and I knew Michael had already enjoyed spectacular safari trips. All that knowledge existed outside me, unable to penetrate my fog of limbo, of *just getting through it*.

In the few days between Michael arriving and all of us leaving, there was a constant flow of activity. My parents came to visit, we celebrated Cameron's birthday (just a year had passed since the teddy bears' picnic and my realisation that I was pregnant), and we organised a family photo session with the boys' cousins. I'd already supervised the packing of yet another shipment of our things, this time from Scotland to Uganda.

The day before we left, friends from the village playgroup came round for a farewell coffee, where they presented me with the plate they had all painted at the ceramics café. It was a surprising moment, and touching, and I was grateful and almost proud of the connections we'd made in my short time there. Having them join me round the table in my father-in-law's house almost made it feel more like home than it had in the nine months up to that point.

And I felt sick.

A knot twisted deep in my stomach. I wanted to relish this last moment of togetherness. But I also just wanted them to leave. I hadn't finished packing. I wasn't ready. I needed to unplaster the friendly smile from my face and get back to gathering and tidying. I already knew I wouldn't be able to leave the house exactly as I'd found it, but I was determined to get as close as possible.

I tried to focus on the moment. My friends were full of questions: *have you seen where you'll be living? How long is the flight? Will you go on safari? Can you drink the water there? What's the food shopping like?* I was off on a big adventure; it was exciting. But I couldn't think beyond the airport. I didn't even know the answers to the questions. I tried my best to answer them with optimism and excitement, all the while thinking, *these are all questions for tomorrow – don't they know that right now I have to pack?*

I hadn't made space for these goodbyes, for the reflection and anticipation. I've learned over multiple moves since, there has to be space for this in the calendar. Otherwise the logistics expand and fill up every available moment before a departure. But this time, the knot twisted and turned in my stomach, grating at the edges. I wanted to be alone, I wanted to create order, organise my stuff, tick off my lists, and I couldn't because of all the people. I wanted them gone.

Finally, they left, and the churning in my gut continued.

I asked myself, is this anxiety? I decided I was experiencing 'proper' anxiety for the first time in my life. I had so often been the optimist, the cross-that-bridge-when-we-come-to-it person. I had dealt with depression, yes, but not anxiety. This was anxiety, I decided. I started to understand how people could talk about anxiety in such debilitating terms. It was a physical, gut-wrenching monster, gnawing away. I couldn't name specific worries. I had honestly felt no particular fear or concerns about moving to Uganda. I wanted the adventure; I knew we would be safe. It was manageable. Yet, there was anxiety – of course there was, who wouldn't be anxious? I was about to live somewhere I'd never even visited, with my two new children. It was just: the unknown.

That night, I had the worst diarrhoea I've ever had in my life, before or since. Worse than in any unfamiliar location.

I spent the night dashing from my bed to the bathroom, over and over again. I seemed to spend hours hunched on the toilet, tears flowing. I'd crawl weakly back into bed whenever I thought my stomach was empty. But it never was. More would come. It was agonizing. My stomach muscles strained and ached. I didn't sleep at all. The whole time, I was thinking, *It's all over!* Surely the flight would have to be cancelled, we'd have to rearrange everything.

By the time light crept into the bedroom, I was a husk of a person, unable to focus or concentrate on anything. I was distraught. Michael told me to stay in bed, try to get some sleep, but I couldn't. I was running through the worst-case scenarios: what if we have to cancel the flights? What if I have to stay here longer? What if I am this ill on the flight? What if the airline staff see my ghostly face at the gate and don't let me travel?

Michael tried to keep me rational while he finished my packing. That itself was a wrench. There had been a plan. There were things around the house that I was supposed to be gathering up, list items I still had to check off. Although I hadn't prepared much at this point for arrival in Uganda, the one thing I'd been in control of was the stuff, the packing, the physical elements of the move – now that was out of my hands too. I was adrift and powerless. He didn't know where everything was. He didn't know about everything that I still had in my head to do.

He told me again to sleep; I told him about the clothes still in the laundry and not to forget that the floppy multicoloured monkey was in the lounge. I just wanted that bit of control back.

Eventually, I slept, just a little, and the onslaught seemed to be over. We could leave for our flight to London. In the business class lounge of Aberdeen Airport, I dolefully popped Immodium, while Michael phoned our driver in Uganda to make sure he'd be there to pick us up.

To this day, I have no idea whether I had some terrible stomach bug, triggered by god knows what, with the worst timing ever...or whether, perhaps, I was literally shitting myself about this move. Did that expression literally mean that this could happen? Could it happen with low-level gnawing anxiety, rather than a sudden adrenaline-flooding scare?

With my body in recovery mode, running on minimum energy, I embarked on my first long-haul flight with small children. I was moving house, moving country, moving continents, to a home I'd never seen before, with a completely drained and empty body, and no sense of control.

The British Airways flight from Heathrow to Entebbe was my first ever business class flight. I refused the champagne, pushed the plate of luxury food around after a few bites, started a movie, then dozed off. But I would forever be grateful for that flat bed. Michael stayed awake with a four-month-old and a just-two-year-old while I slept and slept.

Part Three: Laburnum Courts, Kampala

THE KITCHEN SINK

We arrived in Uganda in April 2013, by which time the company had decided Michael's next career move would be the following year. So it was likely we would move on again within fifteen months. But I couldn't think about that on the morning of our arrival in Kampala, as I moved through the airport in a daze, steered in the right direction by Michael and James, our driver. I did my best to meet him for the first time by being as friendly and open as possible, but despite my long sleep on the plane I was still drained.

Sitting in the back of the Toyota Fortuna provided for us by the company, the novelty of a new country and city gave me a gentle surge of extra energy. I watched life bustling around us on the busy road between the airport at Entebbe and the city. I sat up straight at the moment when the car crested an incline, and the view ahead opened up to an elevated panorama of the downtown skyline. I felt an upsurge of excitement, even.

I would see much of the city in the year ahead from the back seat of our SUV – slow in the traffic, but comfortable, safe, locked inside a hard, protective shell, while soft bodies around us perched helmetless on the back of a boda, a child wedged between a mother and the driver, a baby on her back. Or crammed in with other soft-bodied police officers, on the back of a flatbed truck, seated on a bench or hanging from the frame for the tarpaulin. Our driver would push forward, sometimes accelerating, sometimes merely edging, and could only trust that the boda drivers were paying attention and ready to save their own skin.

Company security told us: if we were ever involved in an accident, we were not to stop, but head straight for the police station. In the worst of outcomes, gathering crowds might take justice into their own hands.

It took over an hour to get from Entebbe airport, on the shore of Lake Victoria, to our apartment in Laburnum Courts in Nakasero, right in the middle of the city. I watched boda-bodas buzzing around every corner of the vehicle. These low spec motorbikes were, I would learn, the mass transit system that kept the city moving. By far the quickest way to get to a destination, it was easy to hail one, for maybe a thousand shillings at the time (about thirty cents), jump on the back of the motorbike, and put your life in the driver's hands as he wove expertly among the SUVs and matatus. Our company insurance policy did not allow us to take bodas, but without them the city would have been permanently gridlocked. The matatu was the other public transport option. The distinctive blue-and-white 'taxis' were actually twelve-seater minibuses that brought commuters into the city from the sprawling suburbs.

On the Entebbe road we passed dozens of matatus crammed with passengers on every seat, and even some standing. I craned to watch out the side window when we passed a stalled matatu, its driver and passengers trying to heave the front wheel out of a muddy pothole while market traders and passers-by looked on, shouting suggestions.

I was at last getting a feel for life in our new city.

Then Michael said, 'So, we have a nanny coming tomorrow for an interview with you.' And the surge of energy deflated.

In the weeks before the boys and I could finally join Michael in Kampala, he and I had spoken on the phone about hiring a nanny and housekeeper, despite my fuzzy-headed inability to focus at the time on what was ahead.

'I've got a couple of names,' Michael said. 'I got a recommendation from someone who's just left, and another one from a neighbour here at Laburnum.'

'Don't do anything until I get there,' I pleaded.

'Look, I know you think you don't want it, but this is an amazing opportunity to have help with a new baby! Everyone here has help.'

I looked around 'our' room in my father-in-law's house, the room where I retreated to be alone with my little person, to shed the polite, ever-smiling, grateful facade that I carried around the rest of the house. I was exhausted from a state of limbo, from negotiating my needs in someone else's home, from new parenthood of course, from decision fatigue at my second spell of packing in a year, and from a lonely yearning for solitude.

I sighed. 'I already told you – it's not that I don't want help. I understand we can afford to hire someone. But I'm not ready to make decisions about that now. And I definitely don't need someone full-time. Let me get there, and settle in a bit, and then we can find someone together.'

'Alright. But I'll call them at least, find out more about them.'

I knew that his anxieties, his eagerness to help me prepare, would be alleviated by action. 'Fine. Just don't make any decisions yet!'

I'd soon come to understand the inevitability of this process. A couple of weeks after arriving, while we were having lunch at Kabira Country Club, our waitress could somehow see the sheen of newness on me, and asked, 'Do you need a housekeeper? I have a sister looking for work.' By then I'd already had staff from our compound knocking on our door daily, telling me about their sister, or their aunt, or asking if we needed a driver, because their brother was experienced. When one of our friends didn't hire anyone extra to work for them, the locals didn't understand why she wouldn't share her relative wealth by providing a job.

But that day, as we drove through an entirely unfamiliar city, my own narrow experience shaped my expectations.

Besides, we were living in a serviced apartment. Part of the deal at Laburnum was that there were staff who came every morning to make or change the beds, change the towels, and clean. It was already like living in a hotel. How could I expect more than that in my daily life?

Sarah arrived the next day: serious, reliable, experienced. She was keen to meet the boys; she was attentive and caring. When I asked her what salary she would expect, I noted it down, momentarily confused, and then we agreed on a trial period, during which she would come Mondays, Wednesdays, and Fridays, because I was sure that would be all I needed. But we would pay her full-time from the start.

I checked up on my confusion after the interview. I hadn't yet internalised the currency conversion between Ugandan shillings and sterling, so I was sure

I had estimated the wrong amount. But no – I would have comfortably paid double the salary she asked for without blinking. I wanted to, but we made up the difference with bonuses and 'loans', increasing her salary over time. If we had paid double the expected salary, she would not have reasonably been able to go to a future employer and demand the same. During her time with us, Sarah bought a piece of land and began building her own house.

So I'd agreed to hire her, and I thought I had it all figured out. But I hadn't bargained on how easily I would give in to the privilege.

The following Monday, she started. On the Thursday morning, I stood in a dreary corner of a dreary kitchen, hidden away from the rest of the family, washing dishes. There was no dishwasher.

The kitchen sink was small, with a square of draining board beside it, in a kitchen of dark wood cupboards and surfaces. Most of the other rooms in our ground-floor apartment had wide, generous windows, with open views to the compound and across to the plush green hill of Kololo, where we could watch the sun set behind the hill. But the kitchen was at the back, with a small barred window facing the compound wall, and the room was deliberately set apart from the living area – because it was designed for use by staff.

I reevaluated my expectations. The following week Sarah came every weekday, although I was ready to send her home by the early afternoon, so her days were shorter than most.

With Sarah there, a maid coming every morning, James the driver coming and going during the day, popping in for a drink of water or a snack, and compound maintenance staff turning up in large numbers for unscheduled air-con checks as well as for requested repairs, my weekdays at home were full of other people. It was exhausting, and by three p.m. most days I'd tell Sarah her day was done, she could go home. I'd usually still be telling her up to an hour later, as she insisted on finishing every scrap of laundry before leaving, even when I said I would be happy for her to leave it for the next day. (She'd be even more horrified when I suggested finishing it myself.)

Meanwhile, I was desperate for an empty apartment, for just me and the kids, when I could flop guilt-free on the sofa and switch off. A half-hour of daytime

TV didn't feel like an option when someone else was busy around me, doing my housework.

Early each morning, as the bedroom door clicked behind Michael on his way to work, I would wake under the mosquito net with a gnawing emptiness in my stomach. My days began with a lead-heavy dread I couldn't quite explain. An hour from that door-clicking moment, the doorbell would ring, and I would have to be 'on'. There would be hours ahead of internal negotiation, of second-guessing what I should or shouldn't ask Sarah to do. Hours of keeping a smiling friendly face on show, or else hiding a tearful face behind the bedroom door, because how could I possibly present as unhappy with this life of privilege? Hours of planning my activities in the apartment around keeping out of other people's way, so that the floors could be washed, the ironing done. Hours of explaining to everyone around me where I'm going, why, until what time, what they should do while I'm gone. Hours of putting my preferences aside about how things should be cleaned, with what products, where things should be put away, because letting people get on with things the way they were used to, the way they had always done it, felt more important than imposing my needs on them.

Then there was the other constant negotiation I was doing with myself day in, day out, which was less about my introvert need for time alone, and more about some deep cultural conditioning I was only just becoming aware of.

One morning I had friends over for coffee – Mel came down from her apartment upstairs, as well as other neighbours from the compound who had become important friends. It was casual, easy. Cameron was at a nursery where he went three mornings a week. We sat around while Ben toddled and played on the carpet in the middle of the room, chatting, watching and smiling at his play. It was easy to have the coffee time with friends, and have Ben with me at the same time.

Then he fussed for my attention, pulling himself up at my knee to be held, fed, played with. I lifted him on my lap, making that familiar gesture of leaning my head away from the hands that grasped at my hair, turning between his hand on my face and the conversation with my friends, attempting to concentrate on what they were saying at the same time as paying attention to him.

Sarah stopped what she was doing and scooped him up.

'Oh, it's fine, he can stay with me. I'm happy to have him here,' I said.

'He's disturbing you. I will take him.' And then Ben turned his smiling face to hers, grabbing for her hair instead, giggling as she carried him away despite my ineffectual comments and gestures – anything but actually baldly stating my preference, at the risk of causing offense or conflict.

At other times, I would sit at the desk in the corner of our spacious bedroom, working through the TEFL course I had signed up for in an attempt to get back to my working life. Ben would be amusing himself on the rug beside me, but as soon as Sarah saw I was working, she would worry about him disturbing me.

'Don't worry,' I would say, 'he can play there while I work.'

'Ah but Catriona you are busy,' – I had eventually convinced her to stop calling me madam – 'I like to have him with me while I work, he makes me laugh.' And she would gather him up to play with her while she did laundry. It was her job, after all. It was far more interesting for her to take care of the boys than to do nothing but laundry or dishes all day. I told myself it was kinder to let her look after him than to argue about it.

After a few weeks, I looked for a mums' group to join, mindful of how my playgroups in Pau and in Scotland had turned out to be an essential touchstone in my week, and I thought it would be a good way to spend focused time with Ben. But all I could find in the expat Facebook group was play dates set up for nannies to bring children to. My first tearful moment of culture shock came then, when I understood that there was a whole foreign lifestyle here that I was expected to be part of: not the foreignness of life in an east African city, but the utter strangeness to me of this expat community where it was normal to delegate so much of daily life to staff, normal to have other people around doing intimate family work. I felt both resistant and utterly out of depth, like this was a level of adulting to which I could never aspire.

Eventually my Facebook post got a response from a Danish woman, inviting me to join a group of mums who met once a week with their kids, and I seized on it. She later told me they rarely invited new people in, but she'd acted on an impulse when she saw my post. I was so grateful she did. That group became another touchstone during my time there, offering something closer to my idea of a normal community of parents, and much more besides.

Still, there was some negotiation to come. The first few weeks I would take the boys and go with the driver to the playgroups, which were hosted at home by each member. Most of the mums lived in houses in the suburbs across Kololo and Naguru, gated properties with huge gardens. The gardens in Kampala were incredible – huge plots of land full of lush greenery and tropical blooms. Many families hired a local carpenter to build a playhouse or treehouse to make the most of their outdoor space, and generous terraces wrapped the houses, overlooking expansive lawns.

The goal for these women was to socialise, spend time touching base and catching up while the children played together. We were all mums of young children, but of varying ages and backgrounds. The hosts who had cooks working for them would produce an amazing spread of afternoon tea. I discovered that, as well as the childcare help that the host had around, other mums also brought their nannies.

But the whole point for me had been to leave Sarah behind and have an activity with the boys, so each Thursday afternoon I divided my time between getting to know my new friends, and helping the boys play – in enormous gardens, where they wanted to be pushed around on all variety of wheeled toys, lifted into treehouses, show me what they had built in the sandpit...

The others felt bad watching me play while they enjoyed the tea and cake. Eventually Keri, a South African mum who made the most of her personal trainer, live-in nanny, and cook, said, 'You must bring your helper with you next time. Just relax and enjoy it!'

Another negotiation. I already felt guilty about leaving Sarah behind with the laundry when I knew she would love to be out and about with us. I felt guilty about interrupting chats with my new friends to run around with the boys. I felt more guilt about the thought of delegating attention to my kids for another portion of the week. But I also felt guilty that the nannies who were there, whose job was to look after other children, were helping to entertain mine as they joined in games.

I lined up the options, trying to choose my poison – which guilt would I give sway to this week? Sometimes, the alternative to guilt is resentment – but here, it felt like I resented all the guilt I was supposed to be feeling, and it was a vicious cycle I couldn't get out of.

Sarah started coming with us to playgroup.

At least once a week, I'd have a conversation with my mum where she'd say, 'Make sure you're spending time with them! You only get this time once!'

At least once a month, I'd see a remark in a Facebook group, or in the comment section of an article, saying, 'I don't understand women who get other people to look after their children. Why did they even have them?'

Every few days I'd have someone approach asking if we needed a nanny or a cook or a housekeeper, because someone's sister or cousin was desperate for work.

Every few days I'd hear about women in the UK who hadn't gone back to work because childcare was so expensive they'd be working for nothing. I'd have friends telling me how lucky I was to be able to study and pursue my own goals because of the help we had.

Then I'd have somebody telling me, 'Don't get too used to it.'

My own inner voices reminded me, 'I never wanted to be a full-time parent.'

Then they said: 'Real women look after their own children, don't they? And clean their own house, find time for study and work, fit it all in and don't need help.'

There it was: the deep cultural, patriarchal bias that I couldn't shift.

***

In Pau, in that first playgroup community, I'd had a Chinese friend whose son was about the same age as Cameron. She had come to the playgroup only a few times after he was born, but her mum had come from China to stay with her, and my friend had quickly gone back to her full-time French classes, with the baby in the grandmother's care.

Meanwhile, in playgroup on a Thursday morning, someone said, 'Must be nice, having a full-time babysitter so you can swan off and do your own thing.'

Someone else said, 'She's not even working full time.'

Someone else said, 'It's just for French lessons. Are they even staying here permanently?'

Someone else said, 'She must have stopped breastfeeding,' and tutted.

I can't remember if I was one of those someones, if I said things out loud or just thought them. A lot of us certainly had a default setting: either we were raising our children by ourselves, or we were earning enough money to justify having help to raise our children. That was the way things were done.

One day she invited me and Cameron for a play date with her son. Her mother had returned to China, and I think she had hired someone part time to let her continue studying. Or perhaps she had had to stop, but either way, she was struggling, and lonely.

'All you playgroup mums,' she said to me, 'I don't know how you do it all on your own!'

'I mean, we just have to, don't we?' I said.

'But why? Who says so? Where I come from, the whole family is around you when you have babies, all the time. Even if I was in China, my mum would have moved in with me to help.' She looked at me wide-eyed. 'Why would anyone think this is something you can do on your own? I don't understand it!'

In that moment, I realised I didn't have an answer. Those of us coming from a western culture, especially anglophone cultures – the US and UK – fully believed that we were supposed to be good mothers as a default, and that the definition of a good mother was someone who didn't need help, whose devotion to her children defined her, and who demonstrated that devotion by not caring about anything else. If we were working, it was only because our time had monetary value, otherwise why would we spend our time away from them? We were conditioned by a culture – a cult? – of motherhood as womanhood, of womanhood as solitary strength, a source of everything, in no need of support.

Our culture had convinced us that only women who earned money deserved help as a parent.

No wonder my friend was bewildered. She had left her 'village' – the village that it takes to raise a child – and found no other village on arrival.

Why would anyone think you can do this on your own?

***

That conversation in Pau was one of my first 'matrix' moments, when it felt like I had been given access to some of my cultural coding, and suddenly saw that my 'normal' wasn't actually a default – I could choose whether to hold on to it.

But here in Uganda, I was still a long way from breaking away from it. I could see the village I had around me, but I couldn't escape the matrix yet, couldn't shake off the guilt that came with being caught between cultures. The conditioning ran deep, and the impact on my mental health would soon come to the surface.

THE CAFÉ LIFE

The nights in Kampala made up for the steep learning curve of my days. Those nights often began at our favourite bar, Camel Club, just along the road from Laburnum. Mind you, the first time I went there, I still had a cultural lesson to learn.

Maybe a month after I'd arrived, Michael phoned one Friday afternoon to suggest we all meet for an after-work drink. While I gathered up the boys, James, our driver, dropped Michael and (big) Ben at the bar, then came to pick us up with Mel.

When we arrived, Cameron ran to his dad, while I set down the baby car seat on the floor next to me and sunk into a low-slung chair. I had barely turned to say hello to Ben when I realised someone was beside me unbuckling (baby) Ben from his car seat. I turned back to see a waitress lifting him out and swinging him up to her shoulder with a beaming smile. She was cooing and fussing and full of adoration, and of course he loved the attention. I jumped back to my feet, nervous but smiling politely, my hands fluttering at waist height ready to take him back. But I wasn't about to get him back, and she was about to get a fright.

We barely registered what was happening before she was across the room and halfway through the door to the kitchen, Ben still in her arms.

'Woah! Where are you going? What are you doing?' I was after her like a shot as we all launched into a clamour of shouting.

She turned to face us, half-way through the swing door, her face stricken with shock. 'I'm just going to show him off to my colleagues while you settle down for your drink.' She was uncomprehending of our discomfort as I eased him back into my own arms. I spent the rest of my happy hour juggling child and cocktail and dividing my attention between friends and offspring.

If she learned that day that foreigners get jumpy when you take on unsolicited childcare, I learned more, then and later, about some less-than-familiar cultural values. That more often than not, I can trust the village around me to look after our interests. And that hospitality in Uganda meant every comfort being taken care of, so that the customer can enjoy their drink or meal undisturbed – including keeping children entertained. Which is definitely good for business, when you think about it. Taking a baby into a busy kitchen was probably a step too far, though.

That day didn't stop us going regularly to the Camel Club. It was cool, friendly, and relaxed, and just along the road from our compound. It was probably once a residential home, nestled at the base of a mature Nakasero garden, the dark-wood-furnished lounge open on three sides, lit by handmade lamps and an understated stylish decor. And they served amazing snack plates that could keep us going all night alongside the cocktails and Tusker beer. I've never forgotten the taste of their feta and coriander samosas.

The Camel Club wasn't our only favourite hangout in Kampala. In Kololo, the lush suburb of embassies and diplomatic residences, and location of one of the world's few urban golf courses, Acacia Avenue was the centre of well-heeled nightlife. At Khana Khazana, we ate some of the best Indian food we've ever had. In fact, Kampala's restaurant scene was impressive – very diverse, and very stylish. We ate Thai, Greek, Lebanese, Japanese, French, Ethiopian, West African, and, of course, Ugandan.

The most iconic Ugandan food might be its street food. Kabalagala, the most popular nightlife spot in the city, further to the south, was the best area to try a rolex – not the watch, but an omelette rolled in a chapati with various fillings depending on how authentic it was. Acacia Avenue was the place for an expat to go for a night out that felt familiar and comfortable, but the real Ugandan nightlife happened in Kabalagala and the Ggaba Road.

For us, Kampala had all the potential to be a party city, not just because of the scene, but because of the help on offer. The first time I asked Sarah if she could babysit, at the additional rate we'd agreed when we hired her, she replied instantly, 'Yes, of course Madam.'

I said, 'But are you sure you're free on that night?' Her own daughter was at a boarding school outside the city, but I knew she was sometimes home for the weekends.

'Yes, I will be there, no problem.'

After we'd had this exchange a couple of times, Sarah told me, 'I can babysit whenever you ask me. I'll let you know if I have a wedding to go to.' Weddings or funerals would have been the only thing stopping her from working. I always gave her at least twenty-four hours' notice, usually more, but she was always available, and would often stay overnight if we were going to be late. Between that, and having a driver – contracted by the company to work for us, but also always available to work overtime for the extra we'd pay him – the city was our oyster.

And if we weren't out at a bar or restaurant, one of our friends had a party in the compound, or there was a company gala at the Sheraton, or cocktails at the boss's house overlooking Kololo. If none of that was happening, Ben and Mel would come downstairs from their apartment two floors above us, to drink beers over cards, a movie, or the latest season of *Game of Thrones*.

On weekends, we could take the kids to Mish Mash – a popular bar that also had a large garden with a playground – and Prunes café held its craft market on Saturdays, where we could enjoy brunch and their indulgent cupcakes. The city had a thriving café culture, inspired by the local coffee beans. Now that pregnancies and breastfeeding were behind me, I could dive back into full caffeination, and Ugandan coffee was particularly delicious. At cafés like Endiro, Javas, and 1000 cups I would linger over long perfectly brewed cups – so much more of a pleasure than the tiny bitter espressos we'd left behind in France.

In Kampala, we had so much of the best of city living.

But I was still getting in my own way. The old complaint in Pau, *My life isn't in my control*, still rung like a refrain through my days, in between the fun nights and carefree weekends. I was still focusing too much attention on the things that were not my normal.

THE MOSQUITO NETS

I'd always had romantic notions of a mosquito net over a bed. It conjured images of diaphanous fabric creating soft focus in a film set in a tropical location. Or of a commercial for an Indian Ocean resort, a breeze gently pushing open the net to reveal a view of blue sky, blue ocean, yellow sand, and palm trees. Of waking up to sunshine flickering through the net, a day of beach time or perhaps safari travel ahead, returning later to an impeccably made bed with the net pulled back and tied with a delicate ribbon.

By the time we had lived and travelled in Uganda for a year, I was becoming a discerning expert in the choice of mosquito nets, and none of that had to do with five star resorts.

The nets in each of the bedrooms in our apartment at Laburnum hung from one central hook above the bed. During the day, the maid gathered them together, then tied them in a chunky knot to keep them out of the way of the bed. At night, I would have to clamber across the bed to undo the knot, then drape the whole thing around the corners of the bed to make sure it created a secure enough barrier all the way round. Because it was only attached to the ceiling at the central point, the canopy was like an attic ceiling, only giving full headroom right in the middle of the bed, so that sitting up to read was a tricky experience. I was very conscious that if I leaned against the fabric at all, small areas of my skin would be easy prey for the marauding malaria-carrying insects. When I finished reading, I would either have to lift the net to put the book on the bedside table or just stick it under my pillow.

In Cameron's room, the net was easier to manage. We'd replaced the ho- tel-style bed that Laburnum provided with a cute junior bed, so the net hung generously around it with room to spare, making a fun tent within his room. With the colourful pixel-squared rug, still with us for another move, laid between his bed and some toy boxes, we made at least his room look more individual, less like a hotel.

Meanwhile, over Ben's cot, the net was a cage-like structure we picked up in Nakumatt, the Kenyan supermarket in the Oasis Mall. It worked like one of those pop-up tents with a zipped opening on the side, just about high enough to step through without crawling. Later, we saw cots that came with an attached net, and nets that could fit neatly around a cot mattress, and I wished we had researched that more – but there's no time for detailed retail comparisons when you need to protect your baby from malaria! Ben was four months old when we arrived, so still sharing our room. We manoeuvred our full size cot through the opening in the net-tent, and squeezed between it and the corner of our bed several times a day. Every couple of weeks I would pull up a chair and thread a needle to darn a hole in the net. Some chores can't wait for the next day.

When he reached six months and we moved that set-up into the spare room, we manoeuvred the cot back out of its delicate net cage, moved everything to the other room, and repeated the process, with yet more darning needed afterwards.

Amazingly, in a year in Uganda we never once found a mosquito bite on either of the boys. We were stringent about spraying repellent towards the end of the day, getting them indoors before dusk, and sleeping under nets. For ourselves, we were more relaxed about being outdoors in the evenings – the social life was too good to miss. We sprayed as much as we remembered, and occasionally found bites, but never caught malaria. Prevention was the strongest tool against the disease, and anyone we knew of who caught it while we were in Uganda had been more relaxed about the cardinal rules – usually sleeping without a net, or not bothering with repellent after dark.

Only when some neighbours were leaving did it occur to me, I could change up our mosquito net set-up. We bought their four-poster style canopy net, and set it up around our bed; it almost looked more like that romantic film scene – except that the whole thing was baby-pink with an elaborate frill around the top. But we had a full-height bed space again, and I just had to pull a curtain back to reach that all-important bedside table.

The utilitarian everyday nets we used at home definitely lacked the romance of the more luxurious ones I saw in our travels. In the safari lodge at Paraa, nets hung from a track mounted in the ceiling, so that the sleeping area – bedside table and all – was curtained off from the rest of the room (not that we had to do that ourselves – part of the turn-down service in a luxury hotel). Our most luxurious treat during our time in Uganda was a holiday in an all-inclusive resort in Zanzibar. That four-poster bed had an integrated net, and yes, from that one I could wake up and look out at the Indian Ocean through a gauzy filter.

But otherwise, the mosquito nets I handled every day were an extra chore, to keep tidy, to keep clean, to soak in repellent every few months, to darn, and to maintain as a potentially life-saving tool. I felt I would never get used to how they got in my way, when I wanted to sit up, or put down a book, or get out of bed, or lift my baby as he cried. He went through a brief phase of waking every night at 4 a.m., and I'd be in the spare room wrestling with the net above that bed, so that I could sit under it and rock him, or so we could sleep in that bed together. Keeping him healthy and bite-free even got in the way of comforting him.

Those nets – I didn't want them. And they gathered up all my resentment in their fibres.

***

But since we would leave the following summer, I only had a year of mosquito nets to get through. The problem with my time in Uganda was that I could tell myself, with everything unfamiliar and uncomfortable, 'Just a year of this to get through.'

Instead of adapting to the number of people who now featured in my daily life by figuring out my boundaries and asking for what I needed, I told myself, 'Only until next year,' and continued to resent it.

Instead of making appointments knowing that the 'scheduled' time in Uganda was a rough target and not an expectation, I tried to force my days to fit my own expected schedule, saying that 'next year' I'd get my routine back.

Instead of enjoying the time to relax in a car driven by someone else, I wished for the freedom of walking around a familiar city with efficient public transport where I could be in control. I sat in the car thinking, 'This time next year I can be spontaneous again.'

Instead of confronting my sense of privilege and exploring the ways I could use it to make an impact, I told myself, 'Not enough time – leaving next year anyway,' and stayed mired in guilt.

I held on to all those negative perceptions, kept them hovering around me, like spinning plates, giving each one a twirl now and again to keep it in motion, because if I let it drop and smash around me then maybe I'd get too close with this unfamiliarity – and then I would be smashed out of my comfort zone. There was no need to let the plates drop. I just had to keep them going a little while longer, then they'd be someone else's problem. They were like an agitated barrier, stopping our life in Uganda from getting too close to the real me.

THE BEDROOM DOOR

O ne night, after a few months in Uganda, I was out for dinner with my
playgroup friends. They had become a grounding influence. No matter
how much traffic there might be, every Thursday afternoon I would get in the
car with the kids and James – and eventually with Sarah joining us too – and
we would spend however long it took to get to a house in one of the city's other
suburbs: Kololo, Naguru, or Ntinda. But the journey would be worth it for
a couple of hours with tea and cakes in someone's beautiful garden, with the
children playing and conversation with these women who just got it, who knew
the situation, who were smart and funny and compassionate and where I just
felt seen and known.

But my introvert self had still been holding back for a while, even though I
was aching to be known more deeply by them, aching for that extra thread of
connection that would bind me more tightly in the group.

We were in a restaurant somewhere in Nakasero. I think it was Italian, but it
might just as easily have been a mezze or sushi place. I was there for the company.

A waiter cleared the starter plates. There were seven or eight of us round the
table, confident women making noisy conversation, smiling, at ease, chatting
about their days, their children's schools, their travel plans. I felt like a fraud.
There was a lull in the conversation. I took a deep breath. I was ready to share
more, even if I had to steel myself for a shocked reaction.

'So...I've been seeing a counsellor.'

***

It hadn't taken long in Uganda for me to realise I needed help. But it took a long while for me to get the help I needed.

In Pau, I'd told Michael I thought my life was out of my control.

Since then, I'd spent a pregnancy living in someone else's house, carefully managing, rightly or wrongly, my reactions, my relationships, the way I took up space. And now I didn't feel in control of my home either, with people coming and going all day. Someone else literally took the wheel of our car before I could go anywhere, there were now two under-twos commandeering my days, and by the time I'd arrived in Uganda we'd learned we'd be moving on again within a year.

In between safari trips and nights out, my days felt impotent and empty, like I was floating around among the expectations of everybody except myself. It was a feeling that had quietly, insidiously taken deep root over the previous few years, unchecked and unexamined.

It manifested as a frustrated rage that I even felt powerless to express against anyone or anything except myself, becoming more and more harmful.

But after five years of constant life-changing transition, how could I know what fully functioning looked like any more?

Despite all that, despite how easy it was to attribute my moods to external factors, I was sure there was something wrong chemically, too. I was no longer breastfeeding, so my body was my own again, but I still suspected hormones were bringing a big wooden spoon to the party and stirring everything up.

Before I left Pau, my gynaecologist had given me a birth control prescription for a hormonal pill. It had taken several goes in my twenties to find a pill that worked for me, so I was suspicious that whatever cocktail of hormones I had wasn't the right balance. So my first stop was the GP.

In my late twenties – before Michael, when I was still teaching – I'd had a depressive episode, triggered by a combination of factors that were easy to pick out looking back. But at the time, I saw none of it coming. When everything fell apart, I fled to my home town, where my mum took me to the family doctor, who'd known me since teenage acne dramas, who was a strong advocate for women's health issues, and who was most likely aware of a family predisposition. It took five minutes of her listening to me before she reached for her pad and prescribed SSRI antidepressants – an idea that shocked me, but it was exactly what I needed then.

Here I was, ten years later, trying to figure out for myself what I needed. But I was no longer in my home town, with a doctor who knew the family. I wasn't in Aberdeen with a doctor who'd known my history for a decade. I wasn't even in France with the doctor who'd followed my pregnancy and prescribed my birth control. I was in Uganda, where I'd have to see a strange doctor, to whom I would have to summarise as articulately as possible all those histories, going back three countries. The doctor I'd seen thus far in Kampala was a middle-aged man who quite reasonably specialised in tropical diseases. I wasn't optimistic.

But I was lucky. My appointment this time was with a British woman about my age, who was fully receptive to my concerns about hormones and mental health, even as I instinctively played things down in my standard attempt to be a reasonable person, to not take up too much space, too much of her time. Her first suggestion was a surprise, though. She gave me a sample bottle.

'There's a gut parasite common here in Uganda that can cause the kind of extreme irritability you're describing. Bring me back a sample so we can test for that before looking at your hormones.'

I was stunned. 'Seriously? A bacteria? So, like, bilharzia or something?' My stomach, whatever it was doing to my brain, turned. We were very aware of avoiding the water in Lake Victoria where tiny worms could cause this unpleasant infection.

'Not bilharzia, no, but something similar. And you'd be surprised how often treating it helps people's moods.'

Bemused, I accepted the sample bottle and made another appointment. Those results, as it turned out, were inconclusive, so she prescribed me the treatment anyway, and then a different birth control pill to try.

But it would take months to fully monitor the effect of a change in birth control, and I was impatient to feel better. I had to find a way out of the cycle of impotence, rage, guilt, self-pity, tears, and yet more guilt over the self-pity and tears.

I had had enough of putting myself on the other side of the bedroom door, into the only space in our home where I could justify being alone. With a desk in there, at least I could pretend I was studying. In reality, I'd be tearful and hiding from the sense of not belonging in my own home. In any circumstances, I would prefer to cry alone, to give in to the moment without burdening anyone else, to cocoon myself and let it pass. But there, not only did I have someone else always around to hide from, but that person was working for me, giving me a gift of time that I only seemed to spend feeling depressed. I had no right to feel this way, in all our privilege, knowing that on the other side of the door was someone who worked hard and lived hard to make the best of things, and that guilt just made me feel even worse about myself.

So there I'd be, behind the door, crying silently, feeling the strain of not making a noise, my body tensed and constrained. I knew that even so, she'd see my red eyes, and surely hate me – imagine me thinking that my privileged life wasn't good enough. We'd go on pretending, and finally the weekend would come, and our home would be my refuge again.

That wasn't every day, but the bad days outnumbered the good days, and it had to stop.

I couldn't talk to Michael, and not just because his instinct was to offer an obvious-to-him solution. I was blaming Uganda, and not only could he not fix that, but I was there because of him. I couldn't offload baggage onto him without it becoming his. His happiness was too bound up in mine – I couldn't ask him to listen objectively to everything that was bringing me down without it tainting his own perspective, not to mention triggering his acute sense of responsibility for our lifestyle. His way of helping me could only be informed by what felt good to him. Talking about myself with him could only ever mean talking about us both.

Mel was a constant support; she was compassionate, and let me complain about Uganda. We'd sit together on her balcony, two floors up from our apartment, and look from our vantage point on Nakasero across to the opposite hill of Kololo. But her experience was different; she'd had longer to adapt and had fewer responsibilities.

Advice rang in my ears from an expat I'd met before the move to Uganda. In a conversation about the challenges of culture shock, she said something I still quote to this day: 'Make friends with people who are positive about the place. Avoid the ones who are always negative and complaining – that energy will bring you down.' Mel was patient, but I didn't want to be that negative friend, someone best avoided.

So I needed professional help – someone I could talk to, rant with, direct my rage outwards, someone who wasn't personally invested in how I lived my days.

As obvious as that seems, it was a heavy conclusion to come to for a Scottish girl who grew up not taking up space in the world, playing down her problems. It didn't come naturally to decide to cross the threshold to becoming Someone Who Needs Therapy. Therapy was for people with *serious* problems, or Ally McBeal characters.

The next hurdle was actually getting myself there. I couldn't imagine asking around for recommendations, or worse, just showing up to a stranger randomly chosen from an internet search. Then, if I found someone in the city, I'd have to ask James to drive me to an address (described according to landmarks, without the aid of a postcode) which might mean an hour or more in traffic, trying to avoid revealing where I was really going (because again, I had too much guilt to let our driver think I was anything other than happy with our privileged life in his beautiful country). Anyway, I envisaged a huge sign by the gate when we got there: Kampala Counselling And Psychotherapy For Fragile Privileged White Women Who Can't Cope With A Bit Of Culture Shock Even When You Are All Doing Their Menial Tasks For Them.

Amid my procrastination, the answer came to my doorstep – literally. The owner of Laburnum was developing an on-site spa which would also incorporate various wellness services. The young pilates instructor who already gave classes on-site was setting it up. When we were chatting after class one day, she mentioned she was going to bring in counselling, and I almost bit her hand off. If I could see someone actually in our own complex? I wouldn't have to drive across town or tell anyone where I was going. I just had to walk down the hill and into another building, like I was popping in to see a friend.

I arranged to see the young American therapist once a fortnight.

***

That night at dinner with my playgroup friends, I wanted them to know this thing about me. Perhaps I even wanted some sympathy. I made my announcement, expecting gasps, murmurs of pity, expressions of *I had no idea... What have you been going through?....So sorry to hear that.*

'So...I've been seeing a counsellor.'

My Danish friend next to me said, 'Oh, who are you seeing? I go to Dr so-and-so over in Naguru.'

The woman next to her said, 'I stopped going to therapy, but I've been thinking it's about time I find someone new.'

From another friend: 'Ugh...I could not cope with settling in here without my anxiety medication.'

And so on, round the table, not one person surprised or shocked, each woman revealing the reality of the measures they took for their mental health. My shoulders fell and my smile softened as I listened, hardly anyone's attention on me – but every word lifting me a little more, as I finally saw myself in them.

My fortnightly conversations with a professional were what I knew I needed, and were working to keep the bad days at bay.

What I didn't know I needed was that powerful, startling moment over a plate of pasta.

The Nile

A long with Kampala's nightlife and good food, I learned to enjoy a lot about Ugandan culture: the café life, the village mentality, with everyone ready and willing to help, not bound by a schedule. But the hassles of city life were ever-present. Making sure we had cash was a stressful weekly quest. James and I would drive round a circuit of banks until we found a machine that was functioning, and then I'd cross my fingers that it wouldn't swallow my British bank card.

I gradually noticed the exploitation of Ugandan workers going on around me, by both local businesses and some expat employers. And there were deep-rooted values in Ugandan culture I would never choose to reconcile or adapt to.

In February, we took a trip out of the country, a much-needed break to Europe. Arriving back at Entebbe, we first stopped for an official who checked our yellow fever vaccination cards – if we didn't have a valid one we'd either be turned back or taken into a room in the airport where someone would administer it. Then we queued for passport control. I fidgeted with Ben in my arms, adrenaline making me jittery. Michael's official work permit had been buried in layers of bureaucracy for months, and we'd been travelling in and out on successive tourist visas. Every time we came in, we expected someone to be suspicious.

'Don't worry,' Michael said. 'If there's any awkward questions we just need to call the company. They'll vouch for us and clear everything up.'

I didn't tell him that part of me hoped they would just deny us access, and we'd have to get on the next flight back out. Then life would be simpler. But today's immigration officer questioned nothing, and we were allowed back into our Kampala life.

James met us at arrivals. After our crawl along the Entebbe road, the atmosphere in the city was ominous. The president had just signed into law a new, violently homophobic Anti-Homosexuality Act (later ruled invalid in court). Meanwhile, another new law, the so-called 'miniskirt ban', was provoking groups of men to assault women wearing miniskirts, stripping them in public. The vagueness of the Anti-Pornography Act, which had also been signed into law that month, had highlighted a nasty misogyny in Ugandan society.

And, as if to offer a visual aid to all that hostility, driving through the city streets we saw that every one of the huge billboards that lined Kampala's thoroughfares had been torn down, leaving jagged fluttering shreds of Coca-Cola red and white by the side of Acacia Avenue. James told me the word on the street was that 'they' had ripped down the adverts in protest at an 'unpaid bill' – the implication being that someone's palm had not been greased.

Driving through the gate of Laburnum Courts didn't feel like much of a refuge either. I'd recently tried to advocate for a maid I thought had been unfairly dismissed, so it too was a place of conflict, not somewhere I belonged. My daily life in the city continued to demand internal negotiation and compromise, hour by hour.

But Uganda offered the ultimate of escapes in its beautiful countryside. During that year, 'going on safari' was not a once-in-a-lifetime holiday, but a frequent weekend minibreak. The five-hour drive on bumpy murram roads wasn't suitable for a toddler and baby (who were too young anyway to appreciate and remember the experience) so my first trip out of town to Murchison Falls National Park was a 'girls' trip' – me and Mel, with their driver, Peter.

Mel shared her already-done-it-once expertise as we planned our trip together. I learned that the best time for a game drive was dawn or dusk, when it was cool enough for the animals to be on the move, and light enough to see them. Then I realised that in between game drives, there was nothing else to do but take a long breakfast and head for the lodge pool with a book...maybe take a nap. Our two days at Paraa Safari Lodge would definitely be an escape.

But first we had to cross the Nile.

The Victoria Nile rises from Lake Victoria, and winds its way up through Uganda and South Sudan, becoming the White Nile, to meet the Blue Nile at Khartoum. The advantage of Paraa Lodge was its location on the 'right' side of the Nile, so game drives could start early in the morning before the first ferry crossing.

The first time I met the river, climbing down with Mel from their Toyota, took me by surprise. Moments before, I had been bumping in the back of the car along a murram road through the forest, under an awning of giant spider webs that stretched between trees as if to plug a gap in the forest canopy; suddenly, we had arrived at the ferry stop. I stood at the bank of the mythical river, its waters lapping at my feet, giving the appearance of stillness, but teeming with predatory life.

I inhaled the pollution-free air, the freedom from responsibility, the expanse of the river, and looked across the surface. The other side was close, easy to see. It almost looked like just a short swim across. A log near the opposite bank floated downriver, moving faster than I thought it should in these seemingly calm waters. The undercurrent from the mighty Murchison Falls, just upriver, where three hundred cubic metres of water per second squeezed through a six-metre gap in the rocks, tugged relentlessly and violently in the shallows. Then again, maybe the log was a crocodile, propelling itself towards a sign of movement on the far bank. I later learned that the Nile crocodile was the largest crocodile species, especially the ones in this stretch of water, since they were so well-fed by the thousands of fish tossed around at the base of the falls.

I stood where the water nonchalantly met the dusty land. I couldn't believe I was standing by the banks of the Nile, in the middle of this continent that for most of my life had been such a distant and foreign place. I could reach out and dip my fingers in the river. But I didn't – it was an unnerving guessing game to wonder where movements came from.

Even more unsettling was trying to gauge the distance between me and the hippos which basked by the bank, hidden among long reeds and grasses. The low rumbling echo of their calls wasn't pretty, and almost seemed to resonate in my body, so that I had no perception of how far away they were without seeing them. This I already knew: hippos were actually the most deadly animals on the continent after mosquitoes, despite being herbivores, because they were fiercely territorial, and deployed their powerful jaws when threatened. A fisherman didn't want to make a wrong turn and find himself inside those jaws.

Was there any more evocative river name than the Nile? I knew the geography, but still it was a revelation to touch it here in Uganda. This was the Egyptian river, where an ancient civilisation engineered their agriculture to meet its tides. The river of Moses and pyramids and primary school history projects. The river of elegant colonial cruises with sophisticated murders solved by Belgian detectives. This was the river that, from satellite views, uniquely threaded a green ribbon through the Sahara until it branched out across the delta at the top of Africa, a tree of life. No wonder it was the river of a thousand stories. Here, closer to the source, the Nile was a different animal, divorced from maps and narrative, real and primal.

The next day, across the river, my first game drive in the savannah was everything the popular imagery promised it would be.

Without the river to cross, we could beat other visitors and leave at the earliest possible moment, while it was still dark, maybe five-thirty a.m., so that we could join the animals after they woke up and were still moving around in the cool morning air. There were a few other guests in the lobby at the early hour, grabbing their weak coffee and dry biscuits as a pre-drive pre-breakfast, but it surprised me that other guests stayed in bed a little longer, waiting to go out at a more civilised time. I didn't understand why someone would come all this way for such a singular experience, then decide a couple of extra hours' sleep was more important than catching a leopard sighting. But I certainly didn't complain: it meant fewer cars getting in the way of the landscape.

So we set out in the dark, Mel and I rubbing the sleep from our eyes, the fresh air of the wee small hours adding to the wakening effect of the coffee. Mel's driver, Peter, was with us for the trip, and our UWA (Uganda Wildlife Authority) guide was waiting in the car park to join us. The darkness made us greet in hushed tones, like we were on a thrilling secret mission while the rest of the world slept. We bundled into the car, layered against the chill in hats and hoodies, cameras charged, flasks filled with more of that weak coffee.

We were the only car on the road. We kept our eyes trained on the forest rolling past, but it was too dark to see anything except a lucky glint of reflected eyes. The sky gradually faded from inky blue to a dark indigo, and we could see dim shapes in the emerging landscape that made us sit up – usually bushes. At one point, Peter got excited. 'Look, rabbits!' Some bobtails crossed the road lit by our headlights. He was so happy to show us our first glimpse of Ugandan wildlife I didn't explain that I would see dozens of rabbits on my daily commute to the Aberdeen suburbs. We weren't here for the rabbits.

After thirty or forty minutes, we had left the forested area behind and made our way up a slope as more light crept above the horizon. Then suddenly, we were there.

It seemed we had crested the ridge of the incline just as the sun edged over the horizon. The savannah expanded before us in first light, the orange glow spreading and stretching across the land, as if with each breath it pushed more of its warmth and light across the ground. Grasses and shrubs dotted the vast open plain, and on the far horizon a paper cut-out silhouette of acacia trees framed the scene. It was the wilderness of my imagination, laid out before me, ready to touch.

Later, we saw lions mating on the road in front of us, and a baboon take down an antelope at full speed. We quickly wound up the car window as a cobra reared at us from the side of the track. In one tense moment, Peter turned the ignition on and let the engine idle, waiting for the signal from our guide to say now – now is the moment to get out of the way of the parent elephant who has spent the last few moments watching us closely, who might just decide we're too much of a threat.

We saw – just – a leopard relaxing in a tree, watched a hippo frolic at the edge of the Albert Nile, captured the image of a majestic Ugandan crested crane framed by more of those iconic acacia trees. But that first cinematic savannah sighting, the ultimate moment of privilege, framed it all, and put everything else, all the frustrations of those months, into perspective.

I made that trip two more times; whenever family came to visit, one of us would 'take' them on a safari getaway. My parents did visit, a journey they would never otherwise have considered, and they had the time of their lives. James came into his own, using his previous experience in tourism to become their personal tour guide during their stay, taking them to all the most interesting spots in the city, as well as driving us up country again, for more game drives, and stopping at a rhino sanctuary on the way, where we could trek on foot to admire the only white rhinos in the country, carefully protected from poachers.

When my brother came to stay, I made the trip with him, too. We'd done the early morning game drive, and we were enjoying the lazy late afternoon reading by the pool, while the air cooled and the sun dipped closer to the horizon. The far side of the pool gave way to a terrace bar, built up to overlook the forested greenery that edged the savannah. A family was over there, playing cards. Suddenly, the older children of the family stood up to crane over the railing and look down. I heard someone shout 'Elephant!' We joined them, and there the animal was, right below us, making its way back and forward through the brush that skirted the lodge, grabbing at leaves and branches with its trunk. We watched it for a while, from the perfect distance, a dress circle view of the show, then my brother went to his room and I went back to my lounger to finish my chapter before dusk.

Shortly afterwards, I heard another flurry of activity from the opposite side of the pool. This time, the elephant was making its way up the slope below the terrace, coming closer to the lodge itself. Rangers ushered the family at the bar away from the pool area. I watched, half through the screen on my camera, as the elephant worked its way closer to the terrace, and then eventually appeared right on the terrace itself, drawn by the water in the pool.

With the pool between us, I lingered to admire the elephant's easy dominion over the man-made environment. I wondered if it wasn't the first time it had come to the pool for a drink, although perhaps not when humans were around. The elephant made for the refreshing water and would have settled in for a long drink, but the rangers got their message across with aggressive noises as they impatiently ushered me to a safer distance. The elephant and I both moved away reluctantly, looking wistfully back at more of what we were thirsty for.

THE AUDITION

B ack in the city, there was another opportunity to connect with a deeper part of myself, although I resisted it at first. Around some of the expat shopping haunts, I'd seen flyers for performances by Kampala Amateur Dramatics Society (KADS). Michael had encouraged me to get in touch with them when I'd been too overwhelmed by trying to fit in to my expat mum role to consider it.

But I followed their Facebook page, because I still missed the musical theatre that had been such a big part of my life in Aberdeen. When there was a call for auditions in early 2014, for a production of *Under Milk Wood* that spring, I decided I might just be ready to reconnect with that passion. The timing was perfect, since we'd be leaving in the summer.

I knew no one in KADS. Relying on no prior connection when I showed up to audition, it felt like I was getting to the source again, to that self-reliant autonomy I once so easily reached for (apart from relying on James to know the address and get me there through the city streets).

The venue for the audition was a bar-restaurant with a stage – the performances would take place there in a dinner-theatre style. I passed the bar and pushed through a double door into a large hall with a raised stage at one end. Tall stacks of chairs lined the far wall, and the director sat behind a table scattered with scripts and a sign-up form in the middle of the room. I gave my name and contact details, and took the script extract he handed me to read over at the side of the room.

It was an open audition, so I could watch other hopefuls mount the stage to deliver their audition pieces. There were Ugandans and internationals of all ages, and it was hard to tell whether they all knew each other or some were newbies like me.

When it was my turn, I took a deep breath to steady the jitters from the sudden surge of adrenaline. But climbing the stairs at the side of the stage, I felt at ease – almost at home. I'd never been in this room with these people before, but I knew what to do here; I knew I was in a place I could belong. I delivered the piece, even using the Welsh accent I'd practised, and left the stage smiling to myself. The director may or may not like me for his production, but I knew I hadn't let myself down. Whatever the outcome, I had reclaimed a piece of myself.

Still, it was disappointing that a couple of weeks later I'd heard nothing. I was sure I'd held my own against the other people auditioning, at least enough for a minor role. The courtesy of a 'no thanks' would have been the bare minimum. I had to admit to myself I was partly relieved though – by now, our plans had changed.

Our time in Uganda was ending sooner than expected. The company wanted Michael to take on a role in the Republic of the Congo. The country was another unknown entity, except for what I'd heard from one Laburnum neighbour who'd previously lived in Kinshasa. But that city was in the Democratic Republic of the Congo, while Michael's job would be in Pointe-Noire, in the country known as Congo-Brazzaville, which was safer and more stable than the larger DRC. That neighbour constantly complained about Uganda and wished she was back in Kinshasa; although she found nothing positive about Kampala, it was an encouraging perspective. For all the challenges I'd faced in Uganda, the positive experiences of city and savannah had been life-changing enough to teach me this: 'unknown' didn't mean impossible – it meant infinite possibilities. I could make Congo work.

The Congo job was a career change for Michael, which meant that first – even better – they wanted him to go to Pau for some training. We would leave Uganda in the spring for nine months in Pau: familiar, friendly Pau, where I'd have my house to myself and drive recognisable roads again. The irony of how keen I was to go back was not lost on me, but mentally, I had already left Uganda behind.

Then, at least three weeks after the auditions, a member of the group sent me a message on Facebook. It turned out the director had mistyped my email address. He'd cast me for six of the many small roles in *Under Milk Wood*, but thought I was ignoring my emails. Could I come to rehearsal that week?

I felt sick at the idea they thought I was ignoring them, and that I had let them down. But I felt even more sick now at taking on something new when I had one foot out the door of the country. The performances were just two weeks before our departure date. I couldn't possibly commit to the play and get ready to move. I told them I was no longer available.

But they'd been relying on me. The director offered to shuffle around the casting so I could have fewer roles with less to learn. The flattery of feeling needed convinced me, along with Michael's encouragement that we'd manage the move together. That Sunday afternoon I gave James the address of another unknown location, a school on the other side of town, and showed up for my first rehearsal.

I knew no one, and didn't think I could make friends. I had to become part of a team where I had no existing relationships and didn't know how things were done. It was deeply uncomfortable, and I regretted making the commitment. There was a short, intensive rehearsal period where I still had a lot to learn, even with the reduced participation. I struggled to feel part of things. One of my scene partners, a man who would be my on-stage husband, caught malaria, and I didn't even meet him for the first few rehearsals.

It took until the week before the performance for me to remember why I was there. We got back into the venue where we'd auditioned, my 'husband' finally present and in full health. The intensity and pressure of the last week of rehearsals forged the intimacy that only comes from the special creative process of people making themselves vulnerable for each other on stage.

On the first night, I stood in the wings hearing the hushed sense of anticipation settling over the audience, the backstage darkness charged with the connective, creative energy shared by actors ready to perform, and said to myself,

'Why did I wait so long?' With Michael and Mel in the audience, I could reveal again something of my true self, even in the guise of a character.

Finally, I wished I could stay in this country and shape more of these experiences, deepen these relationships. Even without the opportunity to continue, these weeks of rehearsal had completely enriched my time in Uganda. If I had let my temporary mindset, my focus on the next thing, guide me, I wouldn't have lived those weeks so fully, and so wholly myself.

***

The day before we left, (Big) Ben and Mel came downstairs to help us with the last of our clearing out. Ben was vicariously excited about our move back to France, reminiscing himself about all his favourite hangouts in Pau. He wondered aloud where our first French meal would be. 'Ooh, will you go to Le Berry first? Or get lunch at Jai Alai?'

'Maybe,' I said, eagerly putting myself back into our French lifestyle, 'but I know I'm definitely looking forward to more club sandwiches at Le Garage!'

Sarah arrived to collect the household things we'd set aside for her to keep. She had found another family to work for, through one of my playgroup connections. Ben instinctively reached for her, and she scooped him into her arms one more time, then burst into tears. She had spent every weekday with him for the best part of a year. Ben didn't know what was wrong, of course, but his face dissolved into grief-stricken tears too. Watching them, I wondered what abiding influence that relationship would have, even if he wouldn't remember it.

Part Four: Not Quite the Victoria Gardens Appart'Hotel, Pau

THE DISMANTLED BOOKSHELF

B efore we arrived in Pau, I'd pictured us settling into our aparthotel in the historic centre of Pau – the same one we'd stayed in just before leaving two years before. No more dusty, noisy Kampala traffic, no more complicated negotiation of how to spend my days. We'd stroll across place Clemenceau, we'd go to Le Berry, the town's iconic French restaurant, for that first meal, I'd stop at the market for pastries, and drive myself around Pau's familiar streets in our rental car.

But this time, the company had made our booking at a different aparthotel further out of town, next to a supermarket we knew well, but which was also a construction site, since it was being expanded. The hotel itself was an oblong block that blended in with the modern apartments and student accommodation surrounding it. When we checked in, we were sent to the building next door – identical on the outside, but actually a private apartment building in which the hotel had overflow accommodation. The furnishing was like a student flat: one basic sofa, a dining table screwed to the wall, low beds with a single wall-mounted laminate shelf for a bedside table. There were wine glasses in the kitchen, but no corkscrew.

We arrived on May 1. Probably France's most important public holiday.

We ate dinner in the only place that was open.

Our first meal back in France was at McDonald's.

***

'It'll work out fine, I promise!'

A couple of days later, Michael looked doubtfully at the picture our friend Will had sent me of the solid wood bookshelf he wasn't even selling – he was *giving* it away before his departure from Pau. 'How will we even fit this in the rental car?'

'No problem – we can take it apart, then reassemble it when we get into the house.'

He sighed. 'What a hassle. We can go to Ikea and just get something delivered. And anyway, do we even need this bookshelf? We're only going to be here a few months.'

At that, I bristled, and redoubled my efforts to get us as nested as possible, as quickly as possible, including seizing the chance to take this lovely solid-wood shelving – for free – off Will's hands.

We didn't have time to wait till we got into a house, consider the space, decide what kind of furniture we may or may not need. This second stay in Pau was supposed to last only nine months.

I went round to Will's apartment and collected the dismantled shelves, loading the frame and supports piece by piece into our small rental car. Back at the aparthotel, I unloaded and took it up in the lift to our temporary lodging, stacking the pieces in a neat pile in the hallway, while Michael looked on, rolling his eyes. 'You're going to have to do this again in a couple of weeks, you realise, then build the thing. It's not worth it.'

By now I'd learned enough: from the rugs, from the space in the corner of someone else's house, from the accidental chair, from awkward mosquito nets. I'd learned that I had to make the most of the stay before it was over, to live it fully, and not in a temporary mindset, even if it was only for nine months. So yes, there would be solid wood display shelving in our hallway, wherever that would be. It was completely worth it. We would have a comfortable home, even if it meant selling everything again a few months later.

There would be no dithering over where we would live either. As far as I was concerned, we had already chosen a house before we even touched down, although the company insisted on the usual process of the relocation agency showing us a shortlist of properties.

Coming back to Pau meant we had a ready-made community there. It was less than two years since we'd left, so although others had also moved on, many of our friends were still there. We'd got to know one Scottish family briefly, and I was looking forward to spending more time with them. So I was disappointed when I heard they were leaving just as we'd be arriving. Then, a realisation struck me, and I quickly got on the phone to Michael at the office in Kampala.

'Tell HR we want their house!'

We'd been guests in their green, sprawling garden for a barbecue, and the house had a charming old-Béarnaise style. I'd seen into the ground floor, to a large living area, and since they, like us, were a family of four, I knew there would be enough bedrooms. Done, I thought. I didn't need to see more. For nine months of living, the most important thing was to get settled as quickly as possible. I agreed to buy a job lot of the other family's furniture, and told the company we'd move in...but they insisted on going through the motions. I toured four houses, including that one, before we could move on to the paperwork.

Still, I figured we could be in there within a couple of weeks. But there was a problem: our shipment was still in Uganda. Somebody had missed out some paperwork, but nobody thought to let us know until we chased the shipping company for a delivery date. More waiting, more impatience.

At least three-year-old Cameron could start nursery school, at the school where I had taught during our first stay. Easy, familiar; we could slide right into that new routine. But no: he got some kind of tummy bug. Cue a week or more of messy diarrhoea, as we lived out of suitcases in a sparsely furnished apartment, with another toddler to keep entertained.

I could barely contain my frustration with everyone who was keeping us stuck in this make-do limbo. The relocation company who were in no hurry to complete the lease, the shipping company who didn't seem able to take the initiative, our company who felt no urgency to help us gather the paperwork needed to get our stuff moved more quickly, the gut bacteria that had me showering down my toddler hourly, and running after him with laundry disinfectant and bleach, while he treated the stack of shelving in the hallway like a climbing frame.

This was all wrong – I was supposed to be in control this time! I had figured it all out by now, on my fourth international move. We make quick decisions, and get settled in. We make the most of the fact that this location is familiar to us. We furnish our home without holding back, make it our nest even if only for nine months, because this is still our life, right now. We don't get stuck in a temporary mindset. We treat our home as much as possible as something permanent. We make our nest where we are.

But how could I get on with being a good expat, with being in control, when we were stuck in this limbo? How could I get started with flat pieces of shelving lying on a floor and space to build them in? We were only in the not-quite-aparthotel for a month, but it felt like forever.

PART FIVE: LOTISSEMENT LE HAMEAU, PAU

The Reassembled Bookshelf

We finally moved in. Even if I chose this house on the basis of one barbecue two years before, this was a nest I had chosen for myself for the first time in five moves, since I had left behind my own flat to move in with Michael in Aberdeen. And it was adorable. Although built in the 1980s, it was in a typical Béarnaise style, with wooden-shuttered doors along the length of the living-dining room, looking onto the large garden. The layout was almost perfect: a playroom near the kitchen, and at the top of a small staircase a corridor with three spacious bedrooms – ours in the middle, a child at each end. Each of the boys' rooms had a cute child-sized wardrobe I'd bought from the previous family, and in Cameron's room, next to his junior bed, I laid the rug of colourful squares that had now been with us in three countries.

Why almost perfect?

Just that one little room I still couldn't get used to – the separate toilet. In our Béarnaise almost-dream-house, our upstairs bathroom was huge, with a large empty space that could have housed a luxurious bathtub. And next to it was another tiny toilet cupboard. Downstairs, where there was a bath, where the boys bathed, the actual toilet was across on the other side of the entrance hallway. With one still in nappies, and the other struggling with toilet training, there were way too many trips back and forward between the loo and the bathroom, hoping nothing unpleasant would drip on the floor in between, and way too many afternoons spent squashed into one of those cupboards trying to coax a toddler into a convenient routine.

Otherwise, we couldn't have had a better house to fit our family. And this time, there were no shag rugs. Alongside the standard furniture basics provided by our company, I bought all the storage furniture the previous family had offered for sale, knowing it would fit perfectly and likely fulfil a need. So we had corners filled and shelves for displaying things.

It took an extra trip between the aparthotel to the house to transfer the components of my solid wood bookshelf as well as all our luggage, and a whole day of me putting the puzzle back together again with none of the original assembly instructions. I got out my tools and built something solid and useful for our nest. Even if I didn't know what life to build for myself in this limbo posting, I would build a sense of permanence in our home.

Any time during our stay when I decided we needed something – more storage in the kitchen, for example – I just went straight out and bought it. No more temporary living, no more telling myself our time in this place wasn't worth an investment. We bought the garden swing set and trampoline from the previous family too, and our garden was in constant use from day one.

But I kept a careful note of everything we had spent, knowing I would sell it again within just a few months.

THE CUPBOARDS

C ameron started school as a cute Early-Years three-year-old. Even in that school where I'd worked, with parents I'd shared playgroup mornings in, a community I'd been part of, in a town I knew well, I felt strangely out of place. I'd hover around the school entrance near other mums, who all seemed to have plenty to connect over, to keep a conversation going. From the sidelines I'd observe them pulling away, saying things like 'I'll send an email about that,' or 'See you this afternoon then,' or 'Let me know how it goes,' because they'd have somewhere else to be. Some of them would head to work, others were in workout gear.

All I could think of to say was 'How are you?' and I had nothing else to tell. I would hover on the edges of conversations, with no context for joining in, with the boys tugging at me to move along, but nowhere else to be.

I'd take Cameron to his classroom, where Ben would instantly find something to play on, in, or with. For much of our time there, people would ask, is he not old enough to be here? As a chunky two-year-old, there were kids not much older than him in Early Years, and some of them were smaller. But until the academic year where he would turn three, he wasn't eligible, and so every morning I'd have to coax him out of the classroom, or even catch hold of him before he could run back in through the doors. He couldn't understand why he wasn't allowed to stay and play with the other kids like his brother.

Next door there was a popular crèche where many international younger siblings spent their days. We toured it, but didn't work our way up the waiting list to get a place during our brief stay. I half-heartedly researched other crèches, but just couldn't face the administrative process, in my second language, of registering and waiting for a place for the sake of just a few months of childcare.

Besides, what would I do with my days for those few months? I would hardly be looking for a job. Other than the unlikely situation of just the right teaching job becoming free at the international school, I had no intention of searching for and adapting to a job I'd only have to leave within a year.

***

One September morning, as I made my way out through the airy, glass-walled central hall of the new school building, Ben tugging at my arm to try to get back into the Early Years play area, one of the other mums came alongside me. She had a question: 'Have you signed up for library volunteering?'

The morning bell rang, silencing playground shrieks while children lined up to be taken into classrooms. I took a beat before I answered. 'No. I mean I thought about it, but...' I trailed off, indicating the toddler extending from my arm.

'Well, you should think about it, because we need more people – maybe you could share childcare with someone else with a toddler so you could both take a turn in the library.'

I nodded encouragingly. 'Well, I suppose that's a possibility. I'll bear it in mind.'

I knew that, in reality, being 'busy' with a toddler was no barrier to helping. It was always the busiest people in a community who did the most volunteering. Yet there were others who managed to preserve their time and energy for themselves, guilt-free.

Although I had a fleeting moment of guilt about leaving other parents to spend an hour in the morning reading to children, and helping them choose books, for once, I could dismiss it quickly. As much as I had accepted that I would spend another year not working, I knew I didn't want to give my time and expertise away for free to a school that had once paid me a professional salary.

But with nothing else to focus on, I wondered how I would fill my days.

Eventually I fell in to the idea I might as well show up for the PTA meeting and see where it took me. I fell all the way into a cupboard.

It was a trap. I had set myself a trap that later I would become adept at avoiding, but back then I missed the signs. When the first PTA meeting of the year was announced, I figured I could sit at the back of the room and listen. I pictured a small committee – in fact, I already knew the president – with decisions to make and events planned. Sure they would need other people to help, and I might spare a half-hour here and there, but really I was there to offer moral support, to nod approvingly when the old hands in this community made suggestions, but to not take on too much actual responsibility. I also pictured an opportunity to meet more parents, chat over coffee and cake, and maybe even make some new friends.

On the morning of the meeting, I dropped Cameron off, then Ben and I made our way through the school corridors to find the advertised classroom. I found what I thought was the right door, but looking through the small window I thought I was in the wrong place – there were only three or four women in there. But sure enough, one of them was Astrid, the PTA president, whom I'd met the first time we lived in Pau. 'Hi, I thought this was where the PTA meeting was supposed to be, but...' I trailed off.

'Yes, this is the place! In you come, good to see you!'

I edged through the door and Ben made his way to the colourful play mat at one end of the room, where there were board books and building blocks. I found a seat, but there was no back row to hide in. The desks and chairs were in a U-shape, with Astrid perched on the teacher's desk, front and centre. A few more mums drifted into the sunny classroom, but the full meeting numbered no more than a dozen.

Once the meeting began, I dug myself deeper into the hole, unable to keep my helpful suggestions to myself as Astrid ticked off the agenda items. By the last order of business, I had sealed my fate by presenting myself as someone with sufficient common sense and a bit of confidence. Combined with my inherent sense of guilt, there was no escaping when Astrid announced, 'Right, last item. New committee members!'

I definitely couldn't trust myself to handle money, so I was safe from the role of treasurer. Someone else agreed to take on the time-consuming job of secretary.

'Right, but we need a vice president.'

A few faces turned to me.

'Oh, that's not me.' I gave a high-pitched laugh. 'I've only been here a few weeks. You need someone who knows how everything works here.'

'No, no, that's not an issue.' Astrid dismissed my protests. 'I know how everything works. You'd just be helping me out.'

I was still reluctant. Faces turned to another confident-with-common-sense type, Camila. She was getting ready to move during the year ahead, and didn't want to commit either.

Astrid needed names on paper.

'Alright, how about if Camila and Catriona share the role of vice president? That way, Catriona gets to know what's going on, and when Camila leaves, there's someone else already in place?' Then, in response to my pleading glare, 'Anyway, don't worry! There's no great responsibility or decision-making to do. You'll just be my right-hand women. Right, it's decided then.'

And the trap snapped shut.

Sure enough, Astrid was true to her promise that the role wouldn't require actually taking much responsibility. She wasn't much of a delegator, but she did a lot of organising and decision-making that required multiple meetings, planning, shopping for events, and crafting of gifts.

One job Camila and I took on was reorganising the PTA cupboard, a repository of catering equipment, craft supplies, and donations in a long narrow space, where dusty boxes had been piled in front of other boxes for the previous couple of years, and it was impossible to see what was there without pulling it all out and starting again.

We spent half a day surveying the contents, figuring out what shelving and containers we needed, then arranged to finish the job in a couple of days. As I gathered toys and books to keep Ben entertained while we worked, I reflected again on the non-working, non-toddler-encumbered parents who avoided volunteering and filled their days as they pleased. Not that I expected gym visits, lunches, and an immaculate home to be any more satisfying than this.

Resentment simmered below the surface as I heaved boxes and catered at events. I was starting to understand that volunteering in the school where I'd once been an expert educator might have been a way to fill my hours, but was no way to fill my life.

My other hours in Pau were filled with supermarket visits, playgroup mornings, or on other days, play dates for Ben, and attempting to grab lunch before going home, so that when he fell asleep in the car, he could go straight down for his nap.

While he slept, I'd catch up with dishes, laundry, and tidying, or if I was doing really well, I'd spend some time at the sewing machine I'd bought myself since returning to Europe, repairing clothes or making gifts. When he woke up, it would be time to collect Cameron, then get home for a snack and some dinner prep before going back out to pick up Michael from the office, since we'd decided that for the sake of a few months we'd make do with one car.

In between all that, there was a lot of shit. Literally. Toilet training proved to be a slow business in our family. On an almost daily basis, I'd be running between the bathroom and the toilet, on opposite sides of the hall, transferring dirty pants to a basin or cleaning out a potty or moving nappies around. I cursed the nappies and the ever-present Sanytol laundry disinfectant for their control of my daily routines.

In some ways, I had made peace with the idea of this year of nothing-but-parenting. As much as I missed Sarah and the other help we'd had in Uganda, I was also relieved to have this time to reset and do things for myself. Knowing that this was a role I'd chosen, albeit with a lack of other options, helped me feel more grounded than I had in Uganda.

Still, the rage would return. The narrative I told myself, that I was dealing with someone else's shit, literally, day in, day out, and that I had been doing that for three years, in three countries, was boring and insidious and infuriating. I would direct the rage at dirty pants and nappies, the instruments of my torture. One time, I threw the dirty pants away from me across the tiny toilet cupboard with such force that it caused tendinitis in my arm, which lingered for years. In my shame, to Michael, to the doctor, to the physio, I blamed an enthusiastic game of garden badminton, secretly sure that it was caused by the more selfish act of reckless, inadvertent self-harm.

THE PICNIC BLANKET

Returning to Pau meant I could return to the anglophone playgroup that had first offered me a place to belong as a parent. Cameron was at school, but I had another baby now – this time Ben would be one of the 'big kids' in the group. Many of the faces had changed, but playgroup was still the essential touchstone in my week. There were new friends and deeper connections.

Not all the faces had changed, though. Lisa was still there. We had first met when she was pregnant and new to Pau. I'd just had Cameron, so Laurie sent her my way for information. She'd been part of the playgroup too, and baby Cameron had played alongside her older daughter, Océane. Two years later, she was one of the few people I knew who was still in Pau, and now, Ben and Elodie, almost the same age, were in playgroup together.

The friendship that sparked in our early parenting experiences grew over another shared connection: she was writing a blog and drafting a book, and her ambition inspired me. I'd started a couple of blogs that had never made it past the first couple of posts, but she followed through on every idea that occurred to her: a blog with aspirations to HuffPost, a children's book, the draft of a memoir. I was jealous, not of her success with her work – that was exciting – but of her ambition, and of her single-mindedness in just getting it done, unhindered by doubt or the pile of unfolded laundry in the corner.

I hosted playgroup much more often this time. I was committed to nurturing the group as a way of paying forward what it had given me, as well as to making the most of our expansive house and garden.

In late spring, one of the playgroup families was about to leave, and this time I was the one offering a festive send-off at the same time as welcoming a newly arrived mum to the fold. Someone else brought the cupcakes, and I laid out our bright blue striped picnic blanket, a leaving gift from Uganda, made of traditional woven kikoy fabric, under the shade of the large oak tree that was the focal point of our garden.

Sitting on the blanket with Ben after everyone had arrived, I paused for a moment among the chatter. Our large sun-soaked garden was full of colour and laughter. My homemade party bunting hung from the shutters along the side of the terrace. Children were diving in and out of the red and yellow circus play tent, giggling on the trampoline, and not-so-patiently waiting for their turn in a Little Tikes car.

I realised I wasn't in a hurry to be anywhere else.

Even when there wasn't a playgroup, or a birthday party, the picnic blanket laid out under the solid old tree became a regular feature of our year in that house. Whether for the kids to eat lunch, for Ben to play on, or for a play date while a friend and I drank coffee at the garden bench, that bright blue picnic blanket was there, bold against the green of the lawn.

The winters in Pau were short, but they were definitely wintry. There were snowy days in the garden too, the sharp fronds of the palm trees tinged white, and Pau is a town where it rains a lot. There were indoor lunches, playgroups when we moved the sofas around ninety degrees to make more playing space. When another friend was leaving, I hosted a playgroup with a lunch of soup and sandwiches, mums bustling round the dining table and chatting in the hallway.

But it was on the picnic blanket, in the garden, under the tree that I made an important mindset shift. Having gone all-in on making even a nine-month home feel settled and nested, investing in furniture, keeping a detailed list of every item and its cost ready to be sold on again quickly before we left – none of that truly made the house feel like home, in the end. It was a worthy investment, making our time comfortable, as complete as it could be, but the genuine sense of home happened in the garden, under the tree, sharing the time with friends, or amongst ourselves. That was where we got rooted.

The tree was at the centre of our outdoor life in that house, offering a shady focal point for the picnic blanket, and shade over the terrace on one side, the trampoline on the other. I would also stand at the dormer window of our bedroom, wishing there was a bigger window and window seat right here so I could sit among the tree itself, fully nested in the rooted thing, up among the branches even though it was only the first floor of the house.

The tree was there as the boys delighted in their paddling pool during the stifling summer heat, and as they delighted again in the unusually heavy fall of snow that winter, although Ben was unsure at first. The two-year-old, born on a snowy day but who'd only known Ugandan weather, watched at first from a safe vantage point behind the double doors, as Cameron and I embarked on building a cheerful snowman. Eventually he ventured outside in his Minion-faced beanie hat to throw himself around with the snowballs.

Yes, the tree kept me rooted, both present, able to stay, and able to look forward to the next place. There I would find another tree at the focal point of my community, another tree that would become a place I felt nested outside of the four walls of our address.

THE LAUNDRY

Ironically, after the struggle to adapt in Uganda, I was looking forward to our next move. For once, the company's original plan seemed unlikely to change, and we were still Congo-bound. I anticipated moving to a house on a large plot of land like the ones some of our friends had in Kampala, where I'd hire a carpenter to build a playhouse under, or even in, a large tree that offered a canopy of shade for outdoor living.

Most of all, I was looking forward to the change in my days. The boys would go to a French school, which meant that Ben would start in *maternelle*, like nursery school, from age three, or even earlier. And of course, we'd have help. I'd be ready for that this time, and I'd make sure it happened on my terms, and that I'd have a space of my own, away from whoever else was coming and going in our home.

All of that meant I'd have time – time I was determined not to waste simply by filling it. I would work again.

One morning, as I remember it, I was standing in front of the too-tall wardrobe in our bedroom, holding Ben on one hip, and a laundry basket on the other, although perhaps Ben was following me around, picking up bits of jewellery from my bedside table. I sighed, standing up on my toes just to reach the hangers to hang Michael's ironed shirts, and thinking about the day when I would live in a home where I would get to decide the height of all our storage.

In the previous days and weeks, as I went about these filled-up days, I'd been thinking about the next move, where I'd be able to get it all *right*, of course. I'd been wondering what I would do with those days, what work I would do. I'd wondered whether I would get a teaching job at the French school perhaps, or the small international school, if there was an opening. I had never finished the English as a foreign language course I'd started in Uganda, but that didn't mean I couldn't do it if I wanted, if there was an opportunity. Or perhaps, if there was a demand for it, I would do private tutoring.

I had all those possibilities in mind, but none of them were firing me up. There were a lot of 'ifs' in those options. They depended on the availability of a job, on the demands of other people. I had to wait to get there to see what those possibilities would actually amount to.

Then there was this thought: these were the options that fitted neatly in the box I was already in. The English teacher box: that was where I belonged, of course. It was years since I'd taught full-time, hanging out in staffroom cliques and going on end-of-term nights out, marking exams and spending my evenings with Shakespeare's late comedies, yet here I was, applying this noun, this label of teacher, to myself and my identity, by default. I'd made one decision in 1998 to do teacher training. There was a story I'd told – and I'd heard it over and over from other people too: 'You're so lucky! You can be an English teacher anywhere in the world. People always want to learn English.' I ought to be a grateful character in that story, having a label that proved to be so portable. It had never occurred to me to remove the label, to get out of the box.

And now there was this dissatisfaction I hadn't been able to put my finger on. I was going to keep carrying this box with me from country to country, the label stuck on securely, and find a place for it to fit. *If* I could find a place for it to fit. I realised that being able to work, having a portable job description, was not the same as having a career. What if that just meant more filling of my days? More marking time as I shifted between jobs that didn't offer a thread of development?

I was circling around all these thoughts yet again while I awkwardly stretched to pull down a hanger for the next shirt in the pile. That day, I'd already fed Ben lunch, got down on my knees to wipe up the mess, made a failed attempt to get him to nap, dealt with dirty nappies and dirty pants.

The silent conversation continued.

What if I didn't even want to teach any more? I missed having a career; I missed the fact that my work had a goal, a sense of progression, of moving towards something bigger.

There was a glow of an idea under all of this, an ember that hadn't quite sparked into life yet.

I finished hanging the shirts and encouraged Ben to come back downstairs with me, so I could go into the garage and empty the next load out of the washing machine.

A timid voice spoke up:

What if I could do whatever I wanted?

The sudden spark of an idea made me stop in my tracks halfway through the playroom, among the scattered Megablocks and Hot Wheels cars. *What?* What did that mean? I took the idea apart, examined it.

What if I could get out of the box, and start again? What if this life of moving from place to place, as determined by someone else's job, was not a constraint, not beyond my control?

What if it was an opportunity?

What if I could do whatever I wanted?

Suddenly it was crystal clear: I had this freedom, this unique opportunity. The only person saying I had to be a teacher was myself. I'd been thinking the box was for life, or that I was on a path that only went in one direction.

But what a privilege, to not have to pay the bills. So I could reset, find a new purpose for the days, and not have to wait and see if I would fit in anyone else's gaps.

I could do whatever I wanted.

Outside of the box, what would I do?

At first, I defaulted to the same ideas, habit and convention pulling me back on to the path I was already on. Tutoring, proofreading – like marking without the lesson planning – online teaching. But that wasn't quite right. This was a gift I couldn't squander. The chance to start again, a blank slate. I mentally cleared the scribbles from the whiteboard.

This was a gift, and I knew who to give it to. Among the toys and the laundry, I went back and offered it up to my sixteen-year-old self:

'What do you want to do?'

She answered in a heartbeat, like it was the most obvious thing in the world, like, how did it take you so long?

'I want to write!'

THE NOTEBOOKS

I went notebook shopping. Truthfully, I'd done this many times before my moment of revelation, browsing in Cultura and FNAC, the French multimedia superstores, as well as in Pau's charming gift boutiques. I always lingered at the stylish stationery sections, coveting beautiful covers of printed card or tooled leather. But what I admired most was the stack of fresh blank pages inside those covers. Flipping through them brought a thrilling sense of possibility.

This time, I pushed my trolley loaded with groceries from Leclerc, and crossed the *centre commercial* to their culture section. I passed through the book department – I stopped there sometimes, to find my next ambitious French read, but the French preference for plain covers made for an uninspired browsing experience. Today I went straight to the back, to their *papeterie*, where there was always a wide selection of Moleskine, Paperblank, and Leuchtturm branded notebooks, as well as pads with decorated covers to suit all tastes, from impressionist paintings to anime characters.

I ran my fingers over the tactile cover of a simple Moleskine, then felt its pages, smooth and substantial. I pulled on the magnetic clasp of a Paperblank with an antique book effect cover, then reached for a thinner staple-bound exercise book that reminded me of the jotters we used at school. I used to love getting a brand-new one, opening it to the first page, writing a neat title, underlining it with a ruler and adding the date in the corner, telling myself that this time, there would be no mistakes. As a grownup, I already had empty notebooks on the bookshelf at home, waiting for perfect inspiration to strike. I wouldn't write in them until I had just the right idea, with the ideal string of words to express it.

Perhaps that was how I'd been holding myself back each time I'd moved to a new country – certainly, with every move, I'd told myself that here was a chance for a fresh start, a chance to erase the mess and mistakes of the previous location, and get it right this time.

But at school, there had been something even more satisfying than the pristine, brand-new jotter. It was the jotter filled with work, cover to cover, a full term of accomplishment. It was thicker and denser, the pages bulging, dog-eared, folded, and fiddled with. There were doodles in the corners, crossings out, remarks from the teacher, corrections, and redrafts. The jotters full of messy work were the evidence of work done and lessons learned, tangible proof of effort and improvement.

In the stationery section, I reached for an A5 Paperblank with an embossed butterfly design on its hard cover. Iridescent oranges, pinks, purples, and blues decorated the wings of hand-drawn butterflies that wrapped the notebook from edge to edge. I pulled back the elastic loop keeping it closed to look at the perfect blank pages.

I asked myself, *Can I make these pages messy?* I wouldn't become a writer without making imperfect attempts on these pages.

The reality of our moves was the same. My experiences in each new location were informed by how I'd experienced the one before, by the mistakes made and lessons learned. There was no real fresh start. Trying to fit in to each new environment, trying to reinvent myself as the perfect expat, was like pretending that nothing had come before.

I paid for the butterfly notebook and took it home, knowing I wouldn't fill it with perfect words, but with bad sentences and scribblings out, the intimations of better writing ahead. None of what came next could happen without what came before, without the first imperfect mark on the page.

THE LUNCH

One of my important playgroup friends was a Scottish woman named Annabelle. She'd previously lived in Venezuela and a friend she'd met there had just returned to Pau from Congo. I invited both women and their children for lunch. With some spring rain in the air, we sat round the table this time, not under the tree, and I picked her brains.

Like every French person we'd met who'd lived in Congo, she'd loved it. 'Oh, you'll have an amazing time there!' The conversation took place in French.

She talked about the compound where she'd lived, which was most likely where we would end up, too. 'There is tennis and a football pitch. The children loved it, didn't you?'

Her two pre-teen kids, a boy and a girl, nodded eagerly.

'How about school?' I asked them. 'Did you like it?'

They laughed. School was another matter. 'Too much homework,' the boy said.

Their mum chipped in, 'But it's a very good French school, excellent teachers, very organised.'

We had already decided that we were going to seize this opportunity to send the boys to the French school in Pointe-Noire. They weren't speaking French yet, and they were young enough to soak it up quickly at school, especially with the support of both parents speaking the language.

She asked me about my work.

I hesitated, but to keep things simple said, 'I'm an English teacher.'

'Oh, with that, you'll work all the time!' she said. 'All the French mums want to speak better English, and maybe you'll get a job at the school as well. Everyone wants to learn English in Congo.' She told me that as a hairdresser, she'd had constant work on the compound.

I asked about the climate.

'It gets hotter in the rainy season, which is like our winter. And when it rains, you have to be ready! There are always flash floods. You need to make sure you always have rain boots in the car for the kids and the driver.'

'So do most people have a driver over there? I wasn't sure if we would need one.'

'Oh, you definitely need to hire a driver,' she said. 'It's essential for parking at the school for pickup. It's absolute chaos there, especially at midi.'

'At midi?' It surprised me that she particularly mentioned lunchtime. 'So most people take their kids home for lunch?'

'Everyone does. The school finishes at midi for lunch. It's only on Tuesdays and Thursdays that there are afternoon classes.'

I tried to reply calmly, like none of this was making me want to reach for the phone to tell Michael to cancel the whole move. I clutched for a fragile straw. 'So on Tuesdays and Thursdays they stay in school for lunch?'

'Not at all. There's no school canteen.'

'Not even packed lunches?'

'No, there's nowhere to eat them. All the teachers go home too – I mean, everyone does, your husband will too – and then on Tuesdays and Thursdays they go back to school at 14.45.'

I was used to the French use of twenty-four-hour time by now. I did a quick sum. 'So the lunch break is two-and-three-quarters hours long?' I honestly think I was blinking back tears at this point.

'Three hours. The morning classes actually finish at 11.45.'

So in Congo, the place where I was going to get my days back, where I was going to have all the time in the world to write, I would only have part-time days for my new/since-I-was-sixteen goals. I half-listened as my new friend talked about what she would do in her mornings to prepare the family lunch, feeling sorry for myself, constrained once again by limitations I hadn't chosen.

THE GARDEN BENCH

O ne sunny afternoon in early July, I put Ben down for his nap. We just had a few weeks left of our time in Pau. I ignored my usual cycle of laundry, dinner prep, Facebook scrolling, and even the never-ending packing and admin list, and made my way out to the garden, coffee in one hand, laptop under my other arm. I set them down on the wooden picnic bench on the terrace, then went back inside to grab a cushion.

It wasn't the most comfortable bit of garden seating. For all my talk of settling in and investing even in a temporary space, the lure of buying a hundred-euro picnic bench from the DIY store rather than a thousand-euro garden set had been too strong. Michael had cursed me when he unpacked each individual plank and screw of the bench, and ended up with blisters from building it.

Still, in the end, we had a cute wooden picnic bench on our terrace, suitably casual and ready for spontaneous garden sitting – just too wooden and utilitarian not to need a cushion.

The bench also offered a different space, away from the laundry and kitchen and packing boxes and visa applications waiting for my attention, with our departure date for Congo now firmly in the calendar. Today, the nap time and bench would serve as 'a room of my own', my attempt to recreate the uninterrupted calm of the writing retreat I had been to the previous month.

It was Michael's idea. I'd told him about my conversation with sixteen-year-old me, about my renewed sense of purpose to pursue writing seriously, rather than my previous nebulous ideas about travel blogging as a hobby, which meant that it never actually happened. It was a relief to free myself of the expectation that I had to be teaching or tutoring. It was liberating to know I didn't have to fit into something predetermined, that I could craft a new career. Writing I would carry with me from place to place, even if I were to take on employment that would suit me as well.

It was a relief for him too, when I finally framed our situation as an opportunity. Yes, I had given up a career to follow him, and he bore that responsibility heavily. But this perspective shift, that I had gained a kind of freedom in return, that thanks to him I could work without thinking about a salary, was liberating for him too.

So he was all in. When my birthday came around, he was pleased with his big idea.

'I found this place in the Loire valley where you can go on a writing retreat. In English. I'll take time off work to look after the boys while you're away.'

'What?' I couldn't get my head around it. He was taking this way too far into the realms of possibility. 'No way. I can't do that! I'm not that kind of writer yet. I don't need a retreat to get writing done.'

'Who said anything about needing it? We can do this, so you should make the most of the opportunity.' He was taking this even more seriously than I had begun to. With all my good-girl conditioning, I expected to do my thing quietly, to fit my writing in to our lives, and not let it infringe on our routine, to not demand anything extra. I already had the freedom not to have to earn money; I wouldn't ask for money to be *spent* on my work. More importantly, I would *never* ask for someone else's time!

But time I got.

Michael had it all figured out already. The five-day retreat for beginning writers ran over a weekend, so he had booked three days' holiday from work to look after Ben and do the school drop-offs and pickups for Cameron.

It felt utterly indulgent, premature (I wasn't a writer *yet*), and selfish (although it wasn't my idea). It was the investment in myself I didn't know I needed. But he did.

On the train north to Poitiers, I opened the butterfly notebook and wrote about how the journey itself, this time alone on a train, already felt like a holiday.

It was a gift of focused attention to develop just one thing. I almost thought I deserved it.

My time at Missé plunged me in to a distraction-free idyll of shedding stifling beliefs about creativity, teasing out ideas from a wide range of sources, and focusing on the skills to express those ideas. With the help of Wayne Milstead, the calm and encouraging writer and teacher at the heart of Missé, I learned something even more important.

I was not a beginner.

I would still have many moments of imposter syndrome. But that retreat for beginning writers was exactly what I needed, because it showed me I was not beginning. I knew the techniques and the craft. I had spent a decade teaching them. I already understood that ideas were not elusive, but in everything, everywhere – I had prompted kids to write something interesting day after day. I had experience that went back to teen-angst poetry and student newspapers, and all the writing I had done every day in my job.

I was already a writer.

I had plenty to learn from Wayne about craft and form and getting out of my own way, but most of all it was that confidence that I came away with.

The next step was to put it into practice – a regular writing practice with words on the page or screen. Before going to Missé, I'd set up a blog with the name I'd had tucked away for a year – The Frustrated Nester. I'd told just one person in Uganda, my counsellor, about that idea: a blog about creating home from place to place in the most literal sense, adapting interiors with temporary fixtures and renter-friendly hacks. But now I would use the name for my writing journey. The night I arrived at Missé, I turned my thoughts from the train into my first blog post and I even hit publish. My first morning there, I woke up with readers out in the world.

But life was no longer giving me solitary train rides and French country houses to write in. Life currently offered moving boxes and uncertainty and chaotic noisy demands on my attention. So I took this moment at the as-yet-unsold garden bench, opened the laptop, and did my best in this pocket of time to recreate Missé, to write with confidence.

A gentle breeze rustled the leaves of my tree. It wasn't sunny, but it was dry and warm. I didn't need extra layers to work outside. Ben slept. I was calm and comfortable and feeling as rooted in my sense of purpose as the tree beside me, regardless of the uprooting transitions ahead.

I wrote.

PART SIX: BÂTIMENT C, COTE SAUVAGE, POINTE-NOIRE

THE CURTAINS

We arrived in Pointe-Noire, the Republic of the Congo, in the early evening. The equatorial sun sets quickly and routinely, so the city was in darkness by seven p.m. But with high humidity, the heat would linger in the air – even inside the airport was hot and sticky, crowded and noisy. On the flight from Paris, I'd wondered which of the other passengers were making the same journey as us, arriving fresh in an unknown country. There was another young family sitting near us, with a freckled mum chasing her red-headed toddler up and down the aisles. Since they, like us, were sitting in business class, it seemed likely they were travelling on a company ticket.

Michael positioned the boys and me well back from the scrum at the baggage carousel, where dozens of eager porters were airside, touting for custom. The other mum was standing nearby, and when she heard me speaking, she approached me. 'I hear you're speaking English,' she said with an English accent. 'I suppose you've arrived here for the same reason as us?'

My shoulders dropped, and I smiled at the sound of a familiar accent and source of connection. We established we were indeed both moving there with the same company, although for Helen and her family it was their second time living in Pointe-Noire.

'Well that's promising!' I said. 'Must be a good place to live if you've come back for more.'

She paused. 'Um, not too bad,' she said, and gave a noncommittal shrug.

I winced and turned my attention back to Michael, who was firmly rebutting the offers of multiple porters. An HR rep met us in the arrivals hall, and together with the other family and a few more new arrivals, we piled into a minibus, which drove us to our new home. It turned out that Helen, her French husband, and their two boys, would be our neighbours in the next-door apartment building for the next three years.

By now, I already knew that we weren't getting to choose a post-colonial house with a sprawling garden like the ones I'd imagined from Uganda. I'd let go of ideas of luxurious outdoor living, and of hiring a carpenter to make the boys a treehouse, like many of our friends in Kampala had done. Our company had a long-established presence in Pointe-Noire, and already owned two apartment complexes. When Michael visited earlier in the year, he'd seen apartments in both, and expressed a preference for the ones at Côte Sauvage – further from the school but closer to the beach; smaller bedrooms but a bigger living space.

We'd only had one flight from Paris that day, but we were travel-tired, feeling the aftershock of getting ready to leave France, and the chaos at the airport was overwhelming. At around eight p.m., the minibus stopped in front of a concrete apartment block. In the dark and in my fatigue, I could only take in the immediate surroundings. We weaved through parked cars and past a series of grey doors to get to the building's entrance, tucked behind what turned out to be the *local poubelle* – the bin room. We mounted the gloomy stairs to the first floor, and the HR rep (I never met her again) showed us in: to a roomy but sparsely furnished living area, with dark terracotta floor tiles and painted concrete walls, without curtains or rugs.

In the kitchen was our starter pack. Not the as-advertised Ikea new-home kit, just a few random plates and pans from the local market. Because the company already owned these apartments, there would be no temporary accommodation, so they gave us these essentials to get us started, along with basics like milk, bread, and fruit. The HR lady was most proud of the aggressive-looking bunch of flowers she'd added, beaming expectantly at me as she pointed them out, like she'd turned my arrival at this concrete block, this echoing, empty space in a dark, sticky, chaotic town, into the welcome of a five-star resort.

'C'est jolie, merci,' I said, but the spiky, angry red flowers that she called *bec de perroquets* were anything but pretty to me in that moment, even with their injection of colour.

After she left, we unpacked our essentials for the night. I'd done this often enough to know that I was too tired, too overwhelmed with unfamiliarity to pay much attention to my feelings of disappointment and discomfort. I knew that with a night's sleep and the clarity of daylight I'd be able to see that life would be okay here.

We went to bed in polyester sheets under scratchy blankets, in curtainless rooms. I ignored all the impulses telling me 'I can't do this!', and perhaps I dreamed of treehouses and garden sundowners.

***

The lack of curtains, at least, I was ready for.

The next morning, our apartment flooded with tropical sun from the floor to ceiling windows in every room, I hauled eight pairs of Ikea curtains out of our luggage. It's amazing what determination can fit into a few suitcases – just as well we never needed bulky warm clothing.

I'd been in touch with April, a Canadian I'd got to know in Pau, who'd been living here for a couple of years. One valuable insight she passed on was that we'd have to supply our own curtains. Most people got them made by local seamstresses, with fabric sourced from the market. But much as I enjoyed a splash of wax print (it was *kitenge* in Uganda, *pagne* in Congo) I knew I wouldn't want entire walls of the busy, colourful fabric in my home. I'd got Michael to take measurements during his visit, so I knew Ikea curtains would be long enough. I picked out light and breezy ones for the living area and heavier ones for the bedrooms to filter out the morning light, and packed them in our luggage – not in the shipment, because we'd need them on the bedroom windows sooner than the six weeks it would take the shipment to arrive.

I set to work on my sewing project. My machine was in the shipment, but I bought some pins to get them to the right length in the meantime. I was determined to get our concrete box of an apartment feeling like home as soon as possible.

Once our shipment arrived, I could add more of the touches that made it the same family home as we'd had in Pau, twice, and in Kampala. Cameron's colourful rug covered the tiled floor between the beds in the boys' shared bedroom. We had a stylish lamp we'd had made as a replica from Camel Club, our favourite bar in Kampala, and we were still using cute bed linen from the time of Cameron's graduation from cot to junior bed.

For the next three years after I hung those curtains – during which, to be fair, they mostly still had pins holding up the hem – I congratulated myself on that frenzied purchase and the game of Tetris that saw me fitting them in the luggage. There were forty apartments on that compound – all exactly the same. Each time I visited someone, I made the inevitable comparison. Most had locally made curtains, bright and colourful but with dark undertones and prints that dominated the room. And I always returned to mine smugly satisfied with its fresh, modern, light living space.

It was satisfying to make that personal statement in a cookie-cutter space, where all the neighbours had the same blank canvas to start from. I remembered feeling the same way when I first moved into student halls as a fresher at university. Along the corridors of Dunbar Hall in Aberdeen, room after room was exactly the same, with the same basic furniture and bedding. I moved my bed to a different side of the room, upturned a moving box and draped a scarf over it for a bedside table, hung posters, lit candles, and made it my own.

I knew people who really hated life on a compound, with good reason: they felt forced into living the same way as everyone else, and would prefer more privacy and freedom. But disappointment about fantasy treehouses aside, I relished it. I was grateful for the ease of laid-on security, help with maintenance, and instant community. That applied to the people who worked for us, too. Our driver, Luxian, and our *ménagère* (housekeeper) Cendrha, later helped by her sister Laetitia, had colleagues, friends to connect with over lunch and at the end of the day. Everyone was part of a well-established community. Of course, not all compounds are the same, and we never experienced the kind of all-encompassing compound that also includes a school, or a supermarket, that people barely need to leave. But getting to join in as part of something bigger than myself, having the potential support of that institution, that infrastructure...I felt that as a real privilege of my expat life.

For a long time, I'd been sure that the best years of my life were behind me, at university. In my twenties, away from the comforts of student life, I missed the easy campus community, the freedom of intense friendships unaffected by other responsibilities, the scaffold of an institution framing my choices, the sense that everything was possible, because nothing was set in stone yet.

At matriculation, I became part of something bigger than myself. At the freshers' fair, I could cherry-pick my social life; I could find my tribe without having to go out into the world and find them.

Not long after moving into Côte Sauvage, posters announced the 'foire des associations'. On a hot Saturday morning, right on our compound, in front of our windows, was the expat equivalent of a freshers' fair: all the sports clubs and charity organisations associated with our company or the international community in Pointe-Noire set out their stalls. Representatives from the tennis club signed up adults and children for lessons, the bridge club recruited members, and charities outlined the volunteer help they needed. There was a sailing club, and reps from the company social club, which offered a variety of craft lessons. But those were three hours long, which made me wonder – were they just trying to fill the days of spouses?

One table had no posters, fancy flyers, or sign-up sheets. There was just a folded handwritten paper sign at the front saying 'Théâtre', and a neat brunette woman sitting behind it, smiling beatifically. I listened with surging curiosity as the brunette described theatre classes for children to one of my neighbours.

My neighbour moved on, and I asked in French (after saying 'bonjour', of course), 'What age group are the theatre classes for?'

'I start classes at age seven.'

Too old for my boys. 'Oh well, thanks anyway,' I said, and moved away.

But then she said, 'Et pour les adultes...' and she had my full attention again. She planned to start an adult drama group too. I introduced myself and told her I would definitely join. Her name was Florence, and she handed over her little black notebook for me to write my email address in.

She said, 'I'm so happy you want to try it out!' Hearing my accent, I'm sure she wondered if my French was up to it.

'No, I'm not trying it out. I'm joining! No question.' There was something about Florence that told me this would be a group worth joining, and anyway, this was exactly what I'd been secretly hoping for ever since I saw the first poster for the *foire des associations*. I just hadn't dared admit it to myself. I may have had my own doubts about the language, but I could read a script – and this was exactly what I wanted.

It was over a year since I'd rediscovered the creative connection of rehearsal and the thrilling anticipation of waiting backstage in the production of *Under Milk Wood* in Kampala. I'd been waiting for the chance to experience that exhilaration again, and if it had to be in another language, so be it. I would struggle through and level up.

It was because I said a big bold 'Oui!' to Florence that day that I had one of the most rewarding experiences of my life ahead of me, and because of the scaffolding institution of expat life, I had the opportunity literally on my doorstep.

Then there was the ready-made community. After university, I'd desperately missed easy access to new friendships: in halls, in each new class, in clubs. There were always new connections, people were ready for it, looking for their tribe all the time, figuring out who they were and what they liked. Afterwards, there was work and colleagues, and that was it. I had a great time with my teacher friends, but I missed the earlier sense of possibility.

It was exciting and energising to get that back when we first moved to Pau and met Laurie, and Hannah, and then Ben, and so many others.

In Congo, as well as our compound neighbours, and my new theatre tribe, we had Pinc – the Pointe-Noire International Community. I didn't want to rely completely on the English-speaking community in Congo – this was my chance to double down on improving my French – but I also knew by now that to get integrated in a new location, it was worth saying 'yes' to everything on offer, because it could lead anywhere. Better to scale back, once I knew I had made connections, rather than to hold back, feel disconnected and then have to go looking for it. So, just like I said 'oui' to Florence, I said yes to everything Pinc had on the calendar: coffee mornings, book group, dinners, boot camp, kids' events, to post-Pilates coffee at the boutique hotel, even a 'biggest loser' weekly meet-up. (I quickly decided this was not the right time for me to be any kind of loser, but highly valued the intimate chats at each weekly check-in.)

I showed up for my first book group within a week of arriving. I was so new that I couldn't gauge the distance between the host's house and our apartment, despite the map showing it was in the same area, so I asked Michael to drive me there. It took us less than a minute to get to Carrie's large beach side house with the high yellow walls.

The book group had an eight p.m. start time, but I waited till Michael was home and we'd had dinner before we left, imagining a casual evening on the sofa around some wine and nibbles. I arrived about quarter past, hoping not to interrupt a deep literary conversation, and the *ménagère* let me in. I made my way through the hallway, a reception area that faced the large pool outside, a spacious lounge area set around a cosy fire, then finally faced a grand dining room, with seven people sitting around a long table, dinner plates in front of them, large dishes set along the table, and an eighth empty seat. They all watched me approach expectantly, and Carrie said, 'Great, you made it! We can get started.'

My cheeks burning, I apologised profusely. 'I didn't realise there would be a meal! I'm so sorry.' I hadn't even read the book – I was just there to meet people.

But despite the formal set-up and the awkward clash against my expectations, within minutes I felt at ease. Carrie was a host who lavished food and attention on all her guests, no matter the occasion, and her warm, easy Californian manner made me feel welcome and relaxed. I wasn't the only one who hadn't read the book. There was lively debate with mixed reactions to the book (*The Girl on the Train*, I think) but the conversation soon moved on to other topics. That was when all the usual questions flew back and forward across the table:

'Why are you here?'

'How long have you been here?'

'Where else have you lived?'

'How long will you stay?'

'Have you found a doctor, a dentist?'

'Do you need help with the school, with language classes?'

'Have you met Valerie yet? She's Scottish too.'

Ah yes, these were my people. This was where I belonged. I was drawn to Emilia, a young American mum with tattoos and lobe tunnels who showed an intense interest in everything I said. I made an instant connection with always-smiling Jo, English and ready to help with anything.

I didn't know yet which of these connections would lead to deeper friendship, or what accomplishments and new opportunities might come of them. There was always a new sense of possibility in the transient life of an international community.

There were restrictions, too, in the institution. Like I had said to Michael in those early years in Pau, the company still had control of our future and our location – at least for as long as he wanted to follow that career path. We gave up some of our autonomy, couldn't choose exactly the home that was right for us. There might be language barriers, and culture shock, and a fog of disconnection from cultural misunderstandings. We were always watching the clock because time was running out until the next move. And we had to be careful that the institution didn't become a bubble, in which we became so comfortable we lost our perspective.

But the scaffold of expat life, all the safe possibilities it offered, also became a place that felt like home. Still, there was always something to bring me out of the bubble.

THE GATE

The October Toussaint holiday was only six weeks after we'd moved to Congo, so I was not remotely ready to look at another suitcase. It was an easy decision to stay put for the two weeks without school, rather than go on holiday, even knowing that the town would be quieter and more sedate than usual. Our new lifestyle was already a fairly routine and constrained one, with less buzz or diversity than we'd experienced in Uganda. But I preferred a quiet couple of weeks over a day of packing what we'd barely unpacked. Anyway, there was a glimmer of something interesting, maybe even exciting, in the weeks that approached the holiday.

Ahead of a general election the following year, the president had called a referendum on the constitution, seeking to be allowed to stand for another term. There was likely to be protest, at least from younger generations; amongst older Congolese, the memories of civil war were fresh enough for them to live with the inevitability of the president continuing his thirty-four-year hold on power.

So, maybe our Congo life was about to be a bit more exciting.

As the last week of school approached, families started leaving, with many taking advantage of cheaper flight tickets before the holidays. Others considered shipping out, but security experts reassured us there would be no need for evacuation; protests would be minimal and confined to specific *quartiers*. Our company had been operating in the region for nearly fifty years, so we had confidence in the advice.

Still, the mood heightened as contingency plans went into action. In the preceding weeks, extra security gates had been installed in the stairwells of all the company's apartment buildings. Our own building housed a crisis centre on the top floor, with its satellite communications equipment. Of the company's two main compounds, Côte Sauvage was the one further from any likely flashpoints, and right beside the coast, so would make for a better stronghold...if necessary.

We got a few alerts telling us to avoid the market, or even downtown, because of planned protests; nevertheless, employees could still cross town and get to the office. This was also the time when we followed the advice to pack our evacuation bags.

It was an unsettling process. It brought absolute clarity. I had to pare down to the barest essentials, not too much to carry over a sustained period. It had to be a backpack, in case I needed my hands free to carry a child. I packed plenty of spare socks, and squeezed in spare shoes, in case I needed to carry those children through water, from beach, to dinghy, to supply boat, because the airport might be closed. Even though I was in tropical Africa, I packed a jumper, which could be a layer to keep me warm if I landed somewhere it was winter, or as a pillow in case I had to sleep somewhere without a bed. Towels could be blankets or pillows too. A hat each, mosquito repellent, sunscreen, Immodium, paracetamol, sterilisation tablets. I included the truly essential documents, like birth certificates, because whatever was left behind, we might never get back. I included as much water as I could carry and as many non-perishable snacks as would fit in the gaps, and made sure I could bear the weight for a prolonged duration.

Then I pulled the drawstring, snap shut the plastic clasps, stowed away in a wardrobe the bag of potential trauma through which I'd just hypothetically lived, and returned to my actual life, not truly expecting to have to actually grab the bag, thinking I would probably only remember it months from now, when I needed someone's birth certificate.

As tensions rose, some of the smaller western companies in town took action. Without our large compounds and well-established infrastructure, for them it was easier to remove family members from the country, rather than have to look after them in individual villas.

One Friday morning, after everyone was already at work, one of my friends heard a knock on her door. The head of security at her husband's American company had decided that, although the employees would stay and continue working, the families would be evacuated. They would fly out that very night.

She told me afterwards the stories of rushed packing, and urgent requests for someone to look after the dog or cat. She and her kids endured a tearful goodbye with her husband at the airport, wondering when they would see each other again and, in the urgency of it all, imagining the worst. All around them, families clutched each other, suddenly having to put an ocean between them, with no timescale for returning, and no reassurance.

Evacuation was not on the cards for us, however; it was entirely our decision to stay or go. We still didn't want to travel, and trusted the company to evacuate us if things got worse. We thought of ourselves as the stoic optimists, sticking it out, too cool to panic.

About a week before the referendum, the SMS system stopped working, which in Congo was not only the most common form of communication but also a popular way to pay bills, top up phone credit, and send money. The government blamed a technical fault, but it certainly made it much harder for protesters to organise gatherings. Then the internet went down, and the only way to communicate was with live phone calls.

So it took a couple of days before we learned that over at the other company compound, in a more central part of town, residents had heard gunshots from a not-too-distant *quartier*. A few more took their holidays, and April and her family found themselves with very few neighbours left. We offered to have them stay with us – part of me relished the idea of bunking in with another family, finding the spirit of the blitz together, with no internet and just some board games and books for entertainment. But they stayed put, to avoid upheaval to their family of five unless completely necessary.

It was late on a Thursday morning when my guilty frissons of excitement turned to actual fight-or-flight adrenaline pulsing through my limbs.

Now we were midway through the school holidays, and I was chatting with some other mums while our kids played in the compound's play park. It was still the tail end of the cooler dry season, so although the grass was grey and puffs of dust rose with every pounding toddler footstep, it wasn't too hot to be out in the middle of the day. We were bored, and goodness knows we were probably complaining of having to do our own housework, what with the housekeepers and drivers very reasonably keeping to their own *quartiers*.

A car came through the gate, too early for the long lunch break.

'That's strange,' my neighbour said, recognising her car. 'I wonder why he's come home already...'

Then, suddenly, a convoy of Fortuners and Hiluxes streamed into the compound, one after the other, some peeling off to park in front of their respective buildings, the rest all nosing into the spaces in front of our building. A group of senior managers and security coordinators got out, then swiftly disappeared into the building and up to the crisis centre.

As Michael walked towards us from our car, I glanced back towards the compound's entrance. The gate was being shut. I heard myself let out a gasp, and my stomach flipped. I had never seen the gate shut before in daylight. I had never noticed its solid blank whiteness, the way it formed a continuous wall around the compound. We were in, and staying in.

I asked myself, was this exciting enough?

More than enough.

***

The next day, everyone was back at the office. I later learned that the crisis point had come when a large crowd of protesters had advanced close to downtown. There were only about a dozen police officers to hold them back, and protect some of Congo's most influential business interests, but – by various means – they gained the upper hand. Protests continued afterwards in some *quartiers*, but the movement had peaked.

Back in our bubble, my need for excitement had peaked. I was honestly looking forward to the rest of the weekend, restricted by the *ville morte* curfew to stay in the compound and able to have some quiet family downtime.

Saturday morning changed all that.

Ben, two years old, sat at the breakfast table, eating nothing, deflated. Our little joker held a pained expression, accented by tiny frown lines. When Michael put his hand on Ben's forehead, his expression darkened. 'He's burning up!'

That was when I noticed he was uncomfortable turning his head.

'Is your neck sore?' I asked, trying to keep my voice light. He nodded, winced, then burst into tears.

Being good in a crisis, I have been known to underestimate a threat, whereas my husband the pessimist would take our kids to the doctor at the first cough or half-degree of raised temperature.

But this time, no debate was necessary.

We didn't even discuss who would take him to the clinic. Michael knew I was the one who could cope better waiting at home with our older son. He scooped up Ben's health book, the car keys, and a change of nappies, and whisked our boy off to the company clinic through near-empty streets.

I definitely got the better end of that deal. I was someone who watched closely as the needle drew a blood test, and was fascinated by fly-on-the-wall surgery footage, while he looked away squeamishly. But watching my wee boy endure a spinal tap to test for meningitis might have tested my stoicism too far. Luckily, I didn't even know it was happening until after the fact.

Meanwhile, at home, my optimism was certainly being challenged as I tried to keep Cameron entertained. Even as I told myself that no news was good news, it was hard to keep still and focused on one thing at a time.

By the time I got a call, our worst fears were behind us: the doctor ruled out malaria and meningitis, and strong antibiotics were working to reduce the fever. But Ben was to stay in the clinic for further tests and rehydration.

Michael and I agreed to swap places. I went to the wardrobe and pulled out one of our backpacks of potential trauma. The referendum would take place the following day, so the town was still tense, if quiet. Although it was now unlikely, Ben and I might still need it if we had to be evacuated from the clinic. I paused at the thought of leaving the other of our family's two evacuation bags there in the wardrobe. The clinic was close to the compound; even so, those bags that had been packed together could start separate journeys.

I undid the clasps and drawstring. I had new essentials to add, including a plug-in mosquito repellent. April had heard our news and called to offer help. She had one crucial piece of advice: 'Bring a plug-in.' It hadn't occurred to me before, but of course a hospital bed wouldn't have a mosquito net. Ben hadn't entered the clinic with malaria; I certainly didn't want him coming home with it.

When our neighbour dropped Cameron and I off at the clinic, my world became very small, and very quiet, for the next 48 hours.

In his room I found Ben half-asleep in the cot, unable to settle. It was an old-school hospital cot, high off the ground at treatment level, and surrounded by tall cage-like bars. He couldn't toss, turn, or get comfortable without having to readjust the IV tube trailing over the top of the bars from his hand to the drip stand. When he stirred and saw me, he raised his hand mournfully, his eyes half open, to show me the bulbous cotton-bud-shaped bandage his hand had become. 'They put a pipe into me,' he said, then lay back down for a fitful sleep.

There were dressings on his spine, arm, and fingers, from blood tests. He wore hospital-issue pyjamas that were far too big: collar up to his ears, ankles and cuffs turned up multiple times. It had the effect of diminishing him even more, turning our boisterous room-filling toddler into a tired and gloomy tiny person who couldn't even fill his clothes.

After a brief visit, Michael and Cameron went home late on Saturday after-noon, and as dusk fell, so did the curfew. Even with the expectation of recovery the following day, we could not leave the clinic until Monday morning.

Later that evening, the paediatrician arrived with a group of medical staff. Ben was sitting on the bed by now, having woken up desperate to escape from his cage. But that was as far as his energy level had taken him; he wasn't ready to hear a story, play with a car, or even play games on my phone. His sporadic mewling cries were his only response to this unfamiliar sense of emptiness, of having a body drained of vigour.

And when the white coats came into the room, the cries turned to near-screams as he instinctively cowered away from them. The doctor explained that none of the tests had revealed the source of the infection, and that in ideal circumstances they would carry out more blood tests.

He sat by the bed, smiled, and spoke gently to Ben, asking how he was feeling. He tried to take Ben's hand, to reassure him he wasn't there to do anything this time. Ben cowered and whimpered, terrified. At that, the doctor decided. 'Well, we can see that the antibiotics are working to kill the infection. His fever is down. As long as that continues, we can just keep treating him. He is so young to keep having tests.' To this day, the source of the infection remains a mystery.

That night was one of the longest of my life. Freed from the restrictive cot, Ben was not interested in going back into it for any length of time, so he and I slept on the bed together. His sleep was fitful, mine non-existent. Every time he moved, this time we both had to fiddle with the IV line. I couldn't sleep. I'd finished the book I'd brought. The only thing on TV was a French news channel, and there was no internet.

The next day, although still pale and listless, Ben felt better, and rooted in my bag. 'Want to play a game on your phone Mummy.' When it was time to go to the toilet, he walked ahead of me clutching his drip-stand. This time in his pyjamas he cut a comical little figure, pulling the drip stand behind him like some seasoned hospital veteran.

The doctor returned and confirmed the all-clear, but that they might as well keep him on the drip for antibiotics and hydration, since we had to be there anyway. It was a relief, of course, but knowing that we didn't need to be there made the next twenty-four hours stretch into infinity. Whenever Ben was napping, I peered out the high window into the ghostly street, craning for a better view, almost willing something to happen, wishing for some excitement...

But none came. The following day, back in the apartment, we unpacked our bags and returned the essentials to their place in our still-new home. But suddenly, that home felt very settled and real. After just two months in Pointe-Noire, we'd been through what would surely be the worst. As our friends and neighbours gradually returned from their evacuations and extended holidays, we were still there. We'd seen it through, and we were ready for anything.

LA SALLE POLYVALENTE

The French school in Pointe-Noire was big, busy and very French. Every morning, our driver, Luxian, would nose our Fortuna between the dozens of other SUVs jostling for space and find one of his prime parking spots near the entrance. The boys and I would clamber down onto the wide sand-covered pavement (better for coping with the rainy season), pass vendors with baskets of veg balanced on their heads, or bouquets of more of those spiky tropical flowers, enter the gate, and walk across to each of their classrooms, which all had outdoor entrances direct from the playground. Weaving through the groups of French parents all stopping to catch up with each other in animated conversation, I thought to myself, 'I can hide here.'

My French was functional but not-yet fluent, and the school was so big and culturally, essentially French, that I could be completely inconspicuous – I would feel no guilt at not showing up for PTA meetings – La Coop, it was called there, short for *coopérative* – and therefore no heads could turn my way at my common sense suggestions, and no committee role could be thrust upon me. I could stay at my desk and avoid the temptation to fill my days with meetings instead of following my newly discovered sense of purpose.

I would be the anonymous, non-French, outsider parent on the sidelines, and I would be happy to be there, hiding.

But by Christmas, everyone knew who I was.

***

In my new theatre group, the first few weeks were excruciating. I came very close to not sticking with it. But it's probably because rehearsals took place in the *salle polyvalente* that I kept at it. The result was that I finally learned to be at home with my version française.

I hadn't heard the term 'salle polyvalente' before I lived in Pointe-Noire, so although it's common in France, whenever I've heard it since, the phrase has always taken me back to that scruffy building in the Côte Sauvage compound, just down one flight of stairs and a few steps away, opposite our apartment building. It was just like the church halls of countless rehearsals during my life, with a small kitchen with handwritten signs to clean up after yourself, a tiny utilitarian toilet, and a storage cupboard filled with random items that no one would ever throw out, but no one else would ever claim.

It was available for anyone who lived on our compound, or even who was resident in town with our company. This included Florence, so she reserved it for our rehearsals every Monday evening. It was also the place where we celebrated all our kids' birthdays, where we shopped at weekend craft markets, and enjoyed memorable parties that went into the wee small mosquito-y hours.

But I became intimately familiar with it every Monday night. We always rehearsed facing the wall with the strange zebra painting as our 'audience', although sometimes a group would practise in the car park outside, surprising late returners from work in the dark with some booming words of Shakespeare en français. Sometimes I'd run words with a scene partner sitting on the steps outside, or even on the swings in the play park where my kids had been endlessly demanding to be pushed earlier in the day.

We'd set up folding tables and stacking chairs, stack them away again and sweep up at the end of the night. Eventually, I was the one who picked up and returned the key to the guards in their little booth at the gate, so at least I was never late. Frankly, sometimes I resented that extra fifty-metre walk to pick it up from their windowed office at the gate.

In my years of doing drama classes and workshops, on and off since child-hood, I had never been a fan of improvisation. I much preferred having a script. Having to think up my dialogue on the hoof took a different energy; I just never saw myself as creative in that way and hated the pressure to come up with something clever and funny in the heat of the moment. Never mind in my second language.

Improvising in French was far out of my comfort zone. And, because we were a brand-new group of mostly French and Congolese, but also from a few other cultures, and still getting to know each other, we did it every week for about two months. There were a few Monday nights I climbed the stairs back to our apartment thinking, 'This is not for me.' But the following week, I would look out the window, think of Florence, think of the energy it was bringing me, and show up again. I'd surely get a script in my hand, eventually.

After just a couple of weeks, Florence had a surprising suggestion. She was at Côte Sauvage on a Wednesday afternoon, using the *salle polyvalente* for her children's group. By the time she finished and was on her way home, I was pushing Cameron on the swings, at his endless request. She stopped to talk to me. 'I've been thinking about you for a play, because you're English –' she quickly corrected herself. 'I mean, British! I want to put on this production with our young friends.'

She was very supportive of the young Congolese performers who were part of our group – she wanted to help them gain professional experience and earn some money. I felt myself squinting to concentrate on her rapid French, hoping she didn't find it off-putting. I understood that she'd chosen a production of *Le Bon Gros Géant* – Roald Dahl's *The BFG* – and since she liked my accent, she wanted me to play the Queen. I was surprised, given that up till now she'd only seen my stuttered attempts at spontaneity in French, but I was still in 'yes' mode, and keen to please my talented new friend.

So I was deep in rehearsal for *Le BGG* before I fully understood what we were preparing for. She'd pitched it to the French school as a Christmas show to entertain the kids. Every child in the *maternelle* and *primaire* sections would watch it, including my children. We did five performances in a week.

So no, I didn't hide. I got on stage, in front of every child in the school, and became completely recognisable. For months afterwards, I heard children in the playground whispering to their *mamans* – 'Regards la bas, c'est la reine!' They were excited to see 'the Queen' strolling among them. I could no longer feign incompetence in the French language.

One day, a couple of months later, I met somebody new, who asked me after a few moments of chatting, 'C'est quoi, votre accent?' and I glowed with quiet pride. Up till then, people might say, 'Oh, you're not French,' or even compliment me on my ability. But for someone to not even refer to my ability to speak the language, just to pick up on an accent, that made all the difference to me. I was no longer marked out as a learner of the language, recently arrived from somewhere else, but a *speaker* of the language, whose accent merely hinted at foreign origins.

I could now join social conversations without wondering how much I was going to miss. If I didn't get the joke or the cultural reference, I had the tools to demand they explain it to me.

And, most importantly, I no longer tried to be French.

I was learning not only to be at home in the language but also to be myself in the language – to be at home in being a foreigner.

Instead of waiting for my French neighbours to introduce themselves – which they never did because French people much preferred to be introduced – I would walk up to them with a confident anglophone hand outstretched.

When it was lunchtime, and everyone was discussing what they would cook for dinner, I stopped feeling inadequate about my answer being 'pasta', and sometimes a French person would say, 'That's a good idea – I should do something more simple sometimes.'

I stopped feeling embarrassed when my theatre friends teased me about how I read lines with my accent and instead leaned in to the unique quirks my accent brought to my performance.

I realised I didn't have to cook the perfect quiche to bring to a party, because my French neighbours were really looking forward to my 'sandwiches anglais' and sausage rolls.

I'd do my best to follow social protocol at stylish French events, but French people would turn up at Pinc events and relish the informality.

After years of trying to fit in, to avoid offending old French ladies with my gauche informality, and to generally sound like a French person, I'd finally figured it out. I had aspired to Frenchness, to be effortlessly chic, to understand wine, master mealtimes, and sound like a Parisienne. But it turned out my French friends envied our anglophone directness, warmth, and flexibility, the way we could quickly break down social barriers.

It turned out that I could feel most at home abroad when I felt comfortable standing out.

THE TREE

M ost of the time, life in Congo was quiet and unremarkable. There was nothing much to do on the weekends, no easy access to exciting travel. Like from Uganda, we could plan amazing once-in-a-lifetime trips – to Cape Town and Namibia – but travel out of Congo was expensive, and the national parks were less accessible than in Uganda. So from one week to another, all life happened within the limited confines of the town of Pointe-Noire, and the couple of beach restaurants within a day-trip's distance.

Life revolved around a town, a community, a compound, around just one tree, sometimes.

I could see the tree from my study, but I spent more time under it.

It was at the centre of the compound. It might have been a type of ficus, but the biology didn't matter. What mattered was the way its branches spread horizontally from about three metres above the ground, offering a generous canopy of shade for our white painted tables and chairs. What mattered too was the way the trunk wound around itself, so that it was easy to find a foothold for six-year-olds who wanted to sit in its branches.

It was right next to the compound's play park, a handy place to sit when the children weren't making incessant demands to be pushed on the swing. It was outside the salle polyvalente, so when there was a crowd partying inside, it was a welcome retreat for a moment of calm and introspection, perhaps with a bottle of Ngok beer.

Every afternoon from about four p.m, with the hottest part of the day over, our children would play outside, sometimes supervised by ménagères, sometimes by their mums who would gather under the tree to chat. The weekends were quieter: some families went to their *case* – a beach hut up the coast, often a shared rental with one or two other expat families. Sometimes on a Sunday afternoon, I would sit under the tree by myself, sitting on a white chair while the kids played, open a notebook, and doodle with words.

The tree became a place where I found an element of home I'd been seeking for years, without realising it, and in a way that surprised me completely.

It took a few tries, mind you, for me to make it happen.

One Friday afternoon, I prepared myself, meticulously, to be spontaneous. As well as the sunscreen and mosquito spray and bottles of water and snacks I normally brought downstairs to have ready as the kids played, this time I packed a small cool bag with a bottle of chilled wine, some plastic cups, and a shareable packet of crisps.

Under the tree, I leaned the cool bag against a chair, just in case there were enough of my neighbours around that day to suggest a Friday drink. I sat on my own to begin with, but it turned out to be a quiet day. Eventually I was joined by Marina, one of my Indonesian friends, a Muslim, so we chatted and the bottle stayed hidden and corked in the bag until we both went back to our apartments.

I tried again the following week. I didn't want to make an announcement, or send out invitations, or force an 'event' to happen, which would place expectations and prompt questions about 'should we bring...?' 'What time...?' 'How long...?' But I did want to create a kind of expectation – that there would be a point in the week we knew we could show up for, if we wanted to.

Here was a tangible, physical representation of 'home' that I'd been aching to create for years, a steadiness I'd been craving: this predictable point in the week that family or friends convene around, regardless of what the rest of their week has been.

I fully associated this idea with Friday. I'd long given up on the expectation of Sunday dinner. In one country after another, I kept that idea on my weekly meal plan, and the chicken stayed in the freezer, unroasted, until I let go of that tie to Britishness. Our Sundays were too many different things in different countries; our weekends focused on exploring and experiencing, and hours spent roasting meat was too fixed of a thing to focus the weekend around.

Anyway, cultural conditioning aside, it was Friday nights that I associated with belonging. My parents had a regular Friday after-work session with friends, the same friends, in the same place, for literally decades. In my twenties I would tease them about the regularity of these routines, query how the same people could keep each other interested and entertained over thousands of hours.

Still, I often joined them at different stages in my life, and gained a sense of the relief that came on a Friday afternoon, knowing that there, around that table, all would be well.

My own Friday belonging happened as a teacher, with colleagues in the booth at the back of a popular Aberdeen bar. I realised it was the predictability of all those Fridays: no one had to make decisions – someone from the group would always be available to slot into the Friday routine. This was what I craved, among the unpredictability of our globally mobile life. Like a kind of passive self-care, to just be and belong without small talk, introductions, newness and unfamiliarity.

So, the following week I did the same: I propped that small cool bag against the bottom of the tree. And again, there were just nannies supervising, then one other mum appeared and chatted for a little while. I wanted there to be more than just one other person, to have a group to take on this thing together, not a pair under pressure to make the moment count with each other.

A few days later, maybe a Tuesday, I found another route to my goal. The following week was the start of one of the many school holidays. I was with Kristina, a neighbour who was frequently outside with her kids, who was warm and curious and funny and always looking for a night out. She was Russian, married to an Iranian, had lived a long time in francophone countries, and she spoke in an endearing mix of French and English.

'So,' I said, during a lull in conversation which was probably about how our sons in the same class were doing, our travel plans, or the lack of them. I can't even tell you which language I was speaking – we would switch between French and English without noticing. 'So, I was thinking, since next week is the holiday, maybe on Friday afternoon we could celebrate with a drink while we sit here?' I crossed my fingers. 'I could bring down a bottle of wine,' I continued.

Kristina's eyes lit up. 'Oh oui! That is très bonne idée. Moi aussi, je bring vin!'

'Great!' I said. 'We can see who is there on Friday to join us.'

Now I had an ally, and the plan was not a failure, yet.

Kristina said, 'When je vois les autres I will let them know.'

'Les autres' were mostly French, and their enthusiasm was more reserved. Someone said, 'Donc, à 17h?' thinking they were being *invited* to an *event*, which couldn't start earlier than five p.m, because why would you drink before five p.m?

When I said, 'On va voir...si on arrive 16h, ça marche aussi,' she raised her eyebrows and puffed her breath out at my idea that having a drink at four p.m. would work too.

That Friday, I brought the bottle, some cups, and some snacks, and we celebrated the end of a term. My French neighbours may have had to adjust their expectations of 'comme il faut' by sipping at four-thirty, but they happily joined in. It turned out to be a popular disruption.

'We should do this more often,' I ventured, as the sun slid away and bats overhead left their roosts. That was a popular idea too. After the holidays, I made sure each Friday I was ready to serve some wine.

Within a few weeks, we had a well-established routine. We dragged together the tables across the dust to make space for as many people as possible. We draped *pagne* for a tablecloth, some friends would bring beers, some wine, there were soft drinks for the non-drinkers, and crisps for the kids. I'd bring popcorn too if I was feeling organised. Eventually, people brought little bowls of *apéro* snacks to make things a little more classy, and candles to ward off the mosquitoes. We would sit and chat, and my French improved even more. Sometimes, friends living nearby or those who'd brought their children for tennis lessons to our compound would come and join us. We would joke that we would have to charge them an entry fee. The tradition continued, and became a well-established fact – the Friday Apéro.

Some weeks, if no one had to be anywhere else, the sundowners would keep going down long after sunset, and the working partners (yes, mostly dads) would come home, and as they parked, we'd send the kids off inside, and we'd have just one more.

THE DESK

M y favourite space in our Pointe-Noire apartment was my room. Not my study or office, but *my room*.

We'd already decided we wanted the boys to share a bedroom at this stage in their life, and so we used the add-on space in the L-shaped living area as a playroom. Which meant our third bedroom would be an office – the closed door I wouldn't be hiding behind this time, but working behind. A door I could close on the comings and goings in the apartment, where I could even just sit and read without having to feel self-conscious if housework was going on around me. A privileged space, for sure.

And because the bedrooms were small, it turned out there was really only space for one person's clothes in each room. So with a laptop and pile of books on one desk, the second desk added from the boys' room, where I could keep my sewing machine set up, and all my clothes, accessories and makeup in one place, my 'office' became so much more. I treasured that space; it was like a teenage refuge for a forty-something woman, just without the bed.

A room of my own.

And the mornings, despite my clock-watching frustration as lunchtime pick-up got closer, turned out to be long enough, most of the time. With the quiet routine of Pointe-Noire daily life, if I wasn't at a yoga class or a Pinc coffee morning, I was at my desk, where I wrote: for my blog, or for an online course. I worked through a series of fiction writing courses with a Scottish university, and then I got into a course with Faber Academy, part of Faber publishing. I could keep going on these projects without the sense of urgency I'd felt in the years before Congo, always preparing for a new baby or a new country. We were staying in Pointe-Noire for three years, and that made all the difference.

After the first year, I felt settled and secure enough to take on a role in Pinc that let me stay comfortably nestled at my desk. Having responsibility for communications meant that from behind the introvert safety of my keyboard, I could compile emails, craft social media graphics and updates, make fundraising appeals, and update the membership database. It was a voluntary role that aligned with the work I wanted to do, that added to my sense of purpose instead of filling up my days with busy work. And because Pinc had become such a cornerstone of my life in Congo when we arrived, I was glad to give back to it in a way that didn't take me away from the place I most wanted to be.

To my own surprise, however, that would change. A few months into my communications role, an upcoming committee meeting had me simmering with adrenaline, equally eager and apprehensive about how the conversation ahead might go. The recently elected president, Maureen, had heard unexpected news about her husband's job: she'd be leaving Pointe-Noire much earlier than expected. Pinc needed a new president.

Spending time on the committee had me pretty clued in on what the group needed, and I could already see potential for new ways of reaching out to people. Most of all, I cared deeply about the community, and I wanted to see it develop and grow. When I did a mental roll call of who might be willing and available to take over, there were only two people I wanted to see at the helm, and to my mild alarm, I was one of them.

On the day of the meeting, we arrived at Maureen's house, poured coffee, cut slices of cake, and gathered around her table in a chatter of multiple languages: mostly English, Spanish, and Dutch. With everyone seated, the focus shifted to Maureen as she ran through the agenda of upcoming events and fundraising needs. Then she steered us to the inevitable.

'So,' she said, in her gentle accent, a mix of Scottish and South African, 'this is my last committee meeting, and we need a new president. Who would like to do it?'

I heard myself pipe up, 'I'm willing.' So much for waiting to see if someone else would volunteer first.

Opposite me at Maureen's dining table, Jo volunteered at the same time. 'I could do it.'

We looked at each other, eyebrows raised. Up till now, we had both been the quiet observant helpers, not the leaders.

'Okay,' said Maureen, 'so we have two volunteers. Anyone else?'

Relieved, off-the-hook faces looked back at her.

'We need to vote then.'

Jo and I looked at each other, alarmed. There was no need for an election, no need to find out which of us would get more votes.

'Look, if Jo wants to do it, that's fine by me! I can stand aside,' I said.

But Jo added, 'I think you would do a great job! I would be very happy for you to do it.'

'Well, there has to be a decision,' said Maureen. 'Shall we have a show of hands?'

It was someone else who had the idea that saved us, but I can't remember who I should be so grateful to. 'What if they do it together?

It was the perfect solution. Jo and I beamed at each other.

'Works for me!' she said.

'Now I get to hang out with you even more,' I said.

And that was how the introvert, the helper, the person who'd been told at job interviews she was a manager not a leader, the person who two years before had thought that 'reaching out' was something grown-up, confident, leader-type people did, not her, became co-president of Pinc: a leader, with a vision to take something forward, and pay back to the community.

***

Meanwhile, back at my desk, there was another revelation.

With all the space offered by a longer-term stay, a room to work in, and the long mornings with the boys both in school, I could build some routine in my life.

With my new writer persona, I rediscovered my love of stationery, so as well as gathering a collection of notebooks, both bought and gifted, I went back to using a paper diary instead of trying to fit my life into a digital calendar.

In a weighty black Moleskine planner, I tracked my moods. With colouring pencils, I filled in a corner of each day in the monthly planning pages according to my moods, which ranged from rage or depression (red) to optimism, joy, or accomplishment (yellow). The satisfying, playful colouring-in process helped me keep the habit going.

After three months, I could finally see how my moods cycled without the background noise of pregnancy, a new baby, breastfeeding, bereavement, an impending move, family separation, temporary lodging, or culture shock.

Not only could I keep coming back to the same space, the same page, to track them, but the days were the same. I could then compare one month to another, and know what my body was doing, that my body, my chemistry, were playing their part.

It might seem like a simple, obvious thing, but for years, I hadn't had access to this simple habit of observation.

For years, I could easily attribute whatever emotional state I was in to something external: *it's because of the pregnancy/the new baby/the bereavement/the culture shock/the stress of the move/the temporary accommodation/the family separation...*

I'd read a lot about how culture shock could affect our mental health. 'Adaptation' was always the goal, or perhaps 'recovery'. Whether it was a voice from inside or advice from others, there was plenty of advice about managing my response to external factors. That was important.

But all along, all those years of transition were also burying the mental health needs that were always there, and always will be, on some level. When I said to myself, 'Well of course I'm depressed, it's the culture shock, I'm out of the honeymoon period but I'll soon be on the upswing to adaptation,' or 'It's the pregnancy or breastfeeding hormones, I'll balance out when that stops,' or, 'Life in this country is too hard, I'll feel better when we move again,' how could I know if underneath it all, my baseline serotonin level was actually too low? Or when *everything* was changing *all the time*, how could I pay attention to how my cycle was affecting me from one month to the next, with no point of comparison?

At my desk in Pointe-Noire, the colours stacked up, month by month, in neat triangles on the calendar pages of my planner. I could see what was happening with my cycle, and what else affected my mood. I wasn't depressed, not like I'd been in Uganda, and nothing like the clinical episode I'd had in my late twenties, but I could see where the bad days fit in to my life. I took measures to ease them, started taking a supplement that would help with my cycle, and another one to target the bad days.

The revelation, the amazing thing that happened, was not just that the bad days got better – but so did the 'good' days. I hadn't even realised that my baseline expectation of my own mental health had dropped to a level that was not fully functioning. Getting back to that level changed everything that I didn't even know needed changing.

My routine Congo life gave me that space, that clarity, to look after myself again.

THE PHONE CALL

I t was late spring of our last year in Congo before we had any idea where we would go next. Michael's career manager scheduled a meeting right in the middle of our holiday in Namibia in May. We set aside that day in our itinerary to leave Michael in the Airbnb in Swakopmund while the boys and I played on the beach and went souvenir shopping. But when we returned, there was no outcome. 'Nobody let me know the guy is ill – there was no meeting,' Michael said. 'I'll get to talk to him again after our holiday.'

As we neared the end of May, with just a month of school left, we still didn't know where we'd be moving to. At least by then, I'd moved often enough to know that it would all come together, even at the last minute.

At that time, my dream destination was Denmark. I was ready for a continental change to northern climes, with changing seasons, a cosy Christmas, and a multi-layered wardrobe. I'd never even been to Denmark, but its reputation for well-designed living and my hours watching nordic noir TV shows heightened its appeal. For a long time, it had only been a dream, since Michael's company had no interests there. Then they bought out a major Danish company, and suddenly Denmark was a possibility, although Michael wasn't sure there would be a role for him there.

The day Michael finally met with his career manager, I went to a Pinc coffee morning. Christine was hosting this time, one of the French members who had joined Pinc to make the most of the relaxed and inviting atmosphere at our events. Everyone knew I was waiting for 'the call' – we were so close to our departure there was no point being discreet. With everyone gathered, I made some announcements about upcoming events, and reminded everyone that they would have to choose a new president. Jo wasn't leaving until later in the year, but had decided to step down before the summer. Then I mingled, but got weary of repeating, 'Yes, we're moving. No we don't know where yet. Yes it's getting close. That's right, we will need to enrol the boys in school. It'll work out.'

Finally, my phone rang, and I stepped outside to speak to Michael by Christine's pool, my finger in one ear to muffle the multilingual chatter from inside.

'Well? What's been discussed? Which job do they want you to do?'

'You're not going to be happy,' he began.

'Oh, okay.' Other than hoping for a European stint this time around, I hadn't built up any expectations. I steeled myself for the worst: maybe Angola? Somewhere in Asia would be good – so many travel opportunities. 'Just tell me!'

'Right. So it is Denmark. But not Copenhagen I'm afraid.'

'What? That's fantastic!' I said. Sometimes Michael went too far with expectation management. 'I just want to live in Denmark. It doesn't have to be Copenhagen. Anyway, it's a small country. Are you happy with the job offer?'

'Yes, definitely. It's a good opportunity. I really thought you wanted to live in Copenhagen.'

'Honestly, I've only ever said Denmark. I'm so happy!'

Back inside, friends had seen I was on the phone, and waited wide-eyed for me to relay the news. The rest of the morning was a mix of 'Congratulations!' and 'We'll miss you!' everyone knowing they too wouldn't be there forever.

We were so well-acquainted with transition, with 'the only constant is change', that we were almost more at home with that than in any one place.

PART SEVEN: GAMMEL FÆRGEVEJ, ESBJERG

THE BIKES AND KITES

We arrived in time for lunch.

After our summer visit to Aberdeen, our move to Denmark was disconcertingly quick. The town of Esbjerg on Denmark's west coast had a tiny airport serving only two passenger routes, one of which was Aberdeen. With our Friday morning hop across the North Sea, in less than an hour we were living in a new country. Even in Pau, the two flights it took to get there from Scotland meant setting aside a full day for travel. The sudden shift from one home to another felt breathless, like the opposite of jetlag.

We squeezed ourselves and our luggage into our small rental car for the ten-minute drive into town. Esbjerg was a newer town than Denmark's better-known tourist destinations, but the centre had a charming feel with its elegant red-brick buildings.

Following the navigation on my phone, we picked up keys for our temporary apartment from a central hotel as instructed. Although we were checking ourselves in, our welcome to Esbjerg was the easiest and most seamless we'd ever had. We had this address long before arriving, as well as a detailed list of its facilities and the wi-fi password. Our contact in the company's Esbjerg office, Marianne, had been through this many times herself, so she understood the importance of easing an arrival.

We unloaded our luggage, took it up in the lift to the top floor of a small modern building, and discovered our new temporary home. It was simple but thoughtfully furnished, comfortable and welcoming, with a terrace overlooking the harbour. The boys' favourite touch of Scandi-style design was the Ikea light fitting hung low above the dining table.

'It's like the Death Star!' said Cameron, now seven, as he pulled relentlessly on the cords hanging from the orb-shaped light, so that its panels opened and closed to spread or reduce the glow around the room.

'It's exploding! I am Luke Skywalker!' shouted five-year-old Ben.

That light fitting wasn't one of the iconic Danish designs that the country was famous for – in the weeks to come I would see a certain Poul Henningsen pendant lamp in dozens of Danish homes, their curtains left open as the evenings darkened to share their *hygge* interiors with everyone. But even the cheap and chic Swedish product was ubiquitous in homes, shops, and offices.

With our cases lined up inside, it was still only 11 a.m. on a hot summer day, the sun splitting a clear blue sky. We walked into town along Kongensgade, Esbjerg's pedestrianised high street – the 'walking street' as everyone translated it there. We stopped in a charming, rustic, cosy coffee shop for refreshing juices, and I pictured myself lingering there for long, non-French coffees. I quickly realised it was actually part of a chain, but it still became a regular hangout.

We walked further until we arrived at Torvet, the main square lined with more red-brick buildings. We sat outside a busy cafe and ordered burgers and the wrong drinks: the boys got glasses of orange juice (*appelsaft*) instead of apple juice (*æblesaft*). The burgers were almost good, except for the unexpected curryish flavour of a *remoulade* dressing. But we were happy and relaxed among Danes starting their sunny summer weekend early.

On our way back, I noticed shop windows showing chic home accessories, hip boutiques – a wide range of chain and independent retailers that offered anything I thought I would ever need. After three years in Congo, the easy access to shops and cafés was a delightful luxury.

Other than a quick supermarket visit for essentials (not *remoulade*), I fought all my instincts to unpack and 'settle in', and let Michael plan a tourist weekend for us. On Saturday, we explored nearby Ribe, Scandinavia's oldest town; we happened upon a jazz festival with outdoor performances in its medieval streets. On Sunday, we took the ferry from Esbjerg to the island of Fanø, hired bikes, and cycled across the island with a picnic to a wide, spacious beach looking out to the North Sea. Cars drove right on to the sand as colourful kites stretched into the blue above, gently buffeted by the west coast winds.

This time, we were going to hit the ground running, make the most of where we were now local, and not end up with a bucket list of missed opportunities. The nesting could wait.

THE COFFEE DATES

After just a few days, an almost instant community formed, right on our doorstep.

'I think I heard that young couple downstairs speaking English,' Michael said one afternoon, as we unpacked shopping in our narrow kitchen.

I frowned. 'Are you sure?' I hadn't noticed. Since we arrived, I'd been giving anyone I passed on the stairs a cheery 'Hej!' Our two-bedroom apartment was in a smart modern block, and was an actual home, not an aparthotel like in Pau, or a company compound like Congo. Some neighbours had chic balcony furniture and pots of mature plants. I was sure that while we were passing through, our neighbours were permanent residents.

The next time I passed the young redhead on the stairs, I said 'Hello' instead. Sure enough, she said 'Hello' back. It might even have been 'Hiya'.

'He was right!' I declared, then explained: 'My husband said he'd heard you speaking English, so I thought I'd say hello.'

'Yep!' She gave me a bright smile. 'Where are you from?'

'We're Scottish.' I'd detected an accent. 'Are you…'

She laughed. 'Yes, we're Scottish too. Which part?'

'Aberdeen.'

'Us too! Well, the northeast of Scotland anyway.'

She and her husband and two very young children had arrived a couple of weeks before us, and, like us, their apartment stay was temporary. Her husband worked for the same company, but on a permanent local contract, so their search to buy a house would likely take longer than waiting for a long-term rental.

'Well, let's get a coffee some time,' I said, putting my foot on the next step up. 'My name's Catriona, by the way.'

'You're kidding...me too!'

My namesake wasn't the only new friend I would make literally on my way to the car park in our temporary apartment.

A few days later, there was a new couple unloading shopping from their car. By now I had figured out our company owned more than just one apartment in the building, and listened in. Sure enough, not only were they speaking English, I heard more Scottish accents. More Aberdeen people, no doubt. The industry Michael worked in meant that most Scottish expats we met had a connection to the city.

I introduced myself to the middle-aged couple, whose children were grownup but had travelled with them for many years in the US, Middle East, and Asia. I shared our country list.

The man, Doug, said, 'So are you from Aberdeen?'

With most new international friends, that recognisable city was the answer I gave. But to Doug I gave the answer I usually saved for Scottish people who might have heard of my small hometown. 'Actually, I grew up in Gourock. It's on the Clyde Coa–'

'You're kidding!' There it was again. The woman, Wendy, said, 'Me too!' And there was suddenly a sense of being known and at home in a whole new way. Sometimes even Scottish people need me to pinpoint Gourock on a map, but here I was in Denmark, with a woman who'd grown up a mile away from me.

Another day, the boys and I were in the apartment, with the kitchen door open onto the balcony we shared with the other two apartments on the top floor. We heard a noise from outside, then a toy car rolled into view along the decking. Ben's eyes widened. A friend?

He peered out onto the balcony, then looked back at me.

'Is there a kid there?' I said.

He nodded.

'Go and say hello then.'

He was shy, but his extrovert soul needed company outside the family, so he took a couple of steps outside without saying anything, then waved at the younger boy who was sitting at the other end with his collection of toy cars.

His new Bulgarian friend didn't speak English yet, but was also happy to see a friendly boy-face. After a couple of days of them getting together on the balcony, I finally poked my head out at the same time as the other mum, and we said hello. I chatted to Polina and learned that they were another family with the same company, newly arrived and looking for their Esbjerg home.

Within a couple of weeks I had three new friends round to sit with me under the exploding light fitting, to share coffee and a long braided cinnamon pastry *kanelstang.*

***

On the boys' first day at their new international school, I dropped them off at their classrooms and followed signs to the PTA welcome coffee in the lobby, then began the familiar process of milling around awkwardly with bad coffee in my hand until I caught someone's friendly eye. By now, I had learned never to assume everyone else knew the territory. Being new meant I had no idea who else was also new and hoping for some hand-holding. I no longer waited for introductions and invitations. I approached a woman with confident energy and a broad smile, and introduced myself. Layla was from Azerbaijan and had just moved from London. We clicked and exchanged numbers.

A cheerful blonde woman stopped me on my way to get more coffee. 'Hi!' she beamed. 'I'm Kimberly, and you're my new neighbour!'

Word had got out that we were the family taking the house along the road from hers, which we'd chosen from a small selection we'd toured the week before. I beamed back and introduced myself. 'How lucky to have a friendly face in the neighbourhood before we've even moved in!' I said.

'Of course,' she said with an Australian accent. 'Anything we can do to help, just ask!' A couple of days later, I had added Kimberly's name as our emergency contact for the school's records.

Inderjeet introduced herself to me as she was refilling my coffee cup – she definitely wasn't new since she was wearing a PTA badge. She smiled with a friendly twinkle in her eye.

'Did you know there's an international day in the town tomorrow?' she said.

'I've seen some posters, I think, but I wasn't sure about going.'

'Oh, you must come!' said Inderjeet, so warmly that I knew she really meant it. 'It's at Torvet. Come and find me at the Indian stall and you can taste my tandoori chicken.'

The next day, Cat (the 'other' Catrina) and I walked to Torvet, she pushing her youngest in his buggy. Among the cultural costumes and national dances from all over the world, I made my way to 'India' as promised, and Inderjeet's face lit up when she saw me. Our friendship was sealed.

***

The following week, with the boys in their new school routine, I sat at the dining table under the Death Star light and opened my laptop. I wanted to write about my first impressions of the town, and capture some reflections of how much I'd learned about our globally mobile life.

None of our pictures hung on these walls; we were living out of suitcases again, but looking around, I realised the distraction-free emptiness of the space left me free to focus on my work. Not only that, but I'd had to wait for nothing and no one to start this work. I was continuing what I'd been doing in Congo. I'd given myself tasks to work on when I arrived: building a Denmark-based readership; finding a writer community; themes I knew I could write about. When people asked me what I was doing here, my first response was, 'Writing.'

I was already building a new community for myself and the family. I'd stayed open-minded, letting go of labels like 'expat wife' or 'Year One mum' – other people didn't want to be identified by those labels any more than I did.

An alert dinged on my phone and I suddenly noticed the time – I'd been writing for an hour. I had to get ready for the coffee date Marianne had arranged with Pia, whose job at the *kommune* – the local council – was to welcome newcomers to Esbjerg. Walking into town, I thought about all the ways other people had made our arrival a positive experience. But I was also much more focused on what was exciting about our move, rather than the challenges. I could have dwelt on not having control of our timeframe, on the language barrier, on what I couldn't find in the supermarket; instead I paid attention to the freedom from responsibility of being in between homes, the chance to geek out over learning a whole new language from scratch, and the best cinnamon rolls I'd ever tasted.

I arrived at another chic rustic-style café for our meeting. Over brunch we discussed more than culture shock or how to find a doctor. Pia explained the resources the kommune had on offer to help with networking and business development. I could already see opportunities here that aligned with my own goals. Pia became a friend too.

Weeks passed as the current tenants in our house – another expat family on the move – had to wait longer for their visas for their next location. Although it was frustrating to not have a move-in date, I was determined to relish our time in limbo. I let go of any impatience to feel more settled, because I was open to this *opportunity* to let myself discover what our life in Esbjerg would become.

After years of trying to get through transition, to get to the other side before life could begin again, here I was finally relishing the transition, appreciating it for its own sake.

THE BED IN THE VAN

Sitting on the faux-leather sofa of our temporary apartment, I felt pretty pleased with myself. I was practising my Danish thanks to the subtitles on an old episode of *Big Bang Theory*. It was a grey Sunday afternoon, but I'd successfully accomplished a big job that day, one that would be important in helping us get settled into our new house. I just couldn't quite shake off the niggling feeling that I'd forgotten something.

Anyway, I'd found a bed, and it was worth the effort we'd gone to.

This was the first time in all our moves we'd had to furnish a house. The company always provided either furnished accommodation, or a set of basic furniture, so our moves were all air freight only.

But in Denmark, the alternative arrangement kicked in: a budget from the company to furnish the house ourselves. It was a privilege, but having the cash was one thing; the time investment to choose everything we would sleep, sit, eat, work, and put a book on for the next three years was another thing altogether.

Luckily, I'd learned enough not to be shy. After we'd chosen our house, I found the current tenant on Facebook selling her car, and reached out.

'You don't know me, but we're moving into your house. We don't need a car, but if you happen to be selling any furniture, please let me know first!'

It was cheeky – nobody likes that feeling of having people literally watching and waiting for them to leave their nest, waiting to take over their life, like a cuckoo. I'd experienced it in France, when a very direct Norwegian colleague of Michael's visited, saying 'Are you leaving? When will you move out?' while I was making the most of two more months of our short second stay there. It wasn't just about the house and its contents. In the end, that Norwegian didn't take our house, but another Scottish family did. A few weeks after we left, the woman appeared daily in my 'People You May Know' Facebook suggestions, as she gradually became friends with all the friends I'd left behind, who were still visiting the same house – but not to see me.

But I dismissed the discomfort, and it paid off. I bought their sofa, beds for the boys, bookcases, and desks, with no tricky logistical arrangements for picking up or storing it anywhere.

But we still had to find our own bed. We like a big bed. We'd had at least a king size in Congo. We couldn't go smaller.

The only way to get a king size bed in Ikea was with the unfamiliar Danish set-up of two single mattresses on a bigger base. We already knew we didn't like this in our temporary place, with a dip in the middle of the bed and mattress that would slide apart. The Danes even favoured two single duvets on a double bed. That was not for us. But to buy ourselves a king size bed with one mattress would cost thousands.

Before I had found a solution, at another PTA coffee morning someone said, 'I don't suppose anyone's looking for a king-size bed?'

'Ooh, I am!' I exchanged contact details with Nicole, and I told Michael about it.

'A second-hand bed? Really?' said Michael. 'There's no way we could get that in the car. We'd need to rent a van just to move it.'

'Hmmm...that's true.' Would it be worth the effort? I arranged to have a look. It was enormous, a field of a bed. I wondered if it would even fit in the small bedroom.

Would we hire a van, do the legwork, risk giving up space to move around the bedroom, for this ultimate of comforts? Or would we keep it simple, focus on the temporary, and risk feeling like students for the next three years with a bed that would never quite be comfortable enough?

Of course, we hired the van.

After picking up the keys for the house on a Friday afternoon, we still had the temporary apartment until Monday morning. Nicole's moving-out day aligned. Michael, with one boy, drove the van out to their former farmhouse surrounded by fields just outside Esbjerg, while the other boy and I followed in our rented car. Nicole was there to greet us with her husband, and the two very tall men just about got the mattress into the high-sided van. I pushed away the thought of how Michael and I would manage at the other end.

At our new Scandi house, empty and echoey but freshly painted, a blank slate for a new life, the furniture I'd bought from the previous tenants had been stacked up on a tiled area of the floor while the wooden floors were sanded. The base of the bed was in two pieces and easy enough to move; somehow the two of us hefted the enormous mattress into the bedroom. To my relief, there was still room for small bedside tables on either side of the bed.

I was glowing. We had a luxurious, solid bed, nothing temporary or make-do about it, and we'd saved hundreds of euros. I couldn't have been more satisfied with our day's work. The next day, while the kids were at school, I would load up the car with our luggage and two months' worth of temporary living to move into the house properly. We had one more night in the apartment.

Michael climbed into the van as I locked up the house. 'Right, see you there,' he said. The boys and I got in the car, and I followed him out of our suburban cul-de-sac back into town.

Relaxing back at the apartment, enjoying the cosy autumn hygge of the late afternoon, while the boys built Lego on the rug in front of me, and I watched *Big Bang Theory*, I still felt like everything was a bit too easy. But after six demanding international moves, I had learned enough to make things easier on myself, to let go of the stress and celebrate the wins. So I tried to let myself relax.

As one episode finished, and the Sheldon marathon on Danish TV continued (some things seem to be universal), I said out loud, 'I wonder what's taking your dad so long?'

And then I realised what I'd forgotten.

Instead of following the van all the way to the rental place, I'd automatically driven back to the apartment and forgotten all about him. It was a good half-hour walk away, and I'd watched at least one whole episode.

But Michael was not a patient man – why hadn't he phoned me ages ago? Why wasn't he letting me know how angry he was? I tried phoning him and got no answer. If his battery was dead, he'd have just had to walk. But what if something else had happened?

'Boys, quick, get your shoes on!' Feeling like an idiot, I chivvied them back downstairs to the car, and drove along the harbour road. 'Keep your eyes out for your dad – he might be walking along here.'

Sure enough, about half-way, there was Michael, with no jacket for this chilly grey day. I pulled over and pre-empted any tirade as he climbed into the car.

'I am so sorry! I don't know what happened! I just forgot to come all the way to the rental place! I went home and was waiting for you like an idiot.'

'How could you forget? We were literally leaving the house to go straight there! I said I would see you there!'

'I know,' I was plaintive. 'My brain just switched off or something.' He laughed, his frown easing. 'Anyway,' I said, 'Why didn't you just phone me?'

'Well, that's the thing...' It was his turn to look sheepish.

He had put his phone down beside him on the passenger seat of the van. When he arrived, he gathered his things, the paperwork, the car keys, locked up the van, and put everything carefully into the key drop box.

He had not gathered his phone. It was still in the van. So after a few minutes of waiting for me to catch up, and wondering where I was, he realised he couldn't even phone me.

'Let's put it down to the stress of the move,' I said.

It was his work phone, so it couldn't wait till Monday morning. We drove back to the rental place, found a contact number, and persuaded them to send someone out and open the key drop box so he could get his phone. The young employee was surprisingly friendly, given that he'd had to come out on a Sunday afternoon to help us, and even refused a tip.

So we had hit the ground running in Denmark, but then, maybe there were still some stumbles along the way.

PART EIGHT: SKORPIONENS KVARTER, ESBJERG

THE NEIGHBOURS

We moved into our house ten weeks after arriving in Denmark. Kimberly, who I'd met at the school coffee morning and lived just two doors down, delivered dinner for us: a full roast dinner, carefully wrapped in foil, along with a delicious chocolate cake. I couldn't believe our luck at having an international family almost next door, neighbours who knew exactly what it was like in our globally mobile culture, who understood the need for insta-friendship.

Kimberly knew dinner would be hard to think about amid unpacking our shipment – in my case, for the sixth time in nine years. I set about displaying photos from our party days in Pau, hanging Ugandan paintings, and finding a place for hand-carved art from Congo. The multi-coloured pixel-squared rug, that first real investment we had made for our home in Pau, was one of the first things I unwrapped, and once again I laid it on the floor beside Cameron's bed, in a room that no longer held cuddly toys and picture books, but a desk for homework, a remote control drone, and buckets of Lego.

Our house could not have been more suburban. We were in a quiet cul-de-sac of a quiet suburb in a quiet town. And in the flatness of Denmark, we were on the same level as everyone else. There was no chance of an outlook, of a view, of a vista, except for those who lived right on the coast. I would call our cosy little house, surrounded by other cosy little houses, the hobbithole. It didn't even have a window looking out the front, where the garage was. Not that there was anything to see; the world did not pass round our loop of red brick. The suburb hunkered low to the ground, and it took a few minutes of walking before we would see any glimpse of a horizon beyond the tiled roofs of the rest of the development. There were even cushioning grassy mounds providing a buffer between the houses and the busy roads beyond, the surrounding bike paths softened by woodland and a canopy of foliage. Sometimes, setting off for the day felt like leaving the Shire for a grand adventure.

And sometimes, it felt like our Danish neighbours were hobbits. During the winter months, I could go several days seeing no one. The Danes loved their *hyggelig* homes, with those stylish light fittings, and during the dark winter months, they tended not to venture far from them.

Still, I think it was early autumn, not long after we'd moved in, when the invitation appeared in our mailbox. It was for a street party the following September – almost a full year ahead of when the invitation arrived: date, time and venue all decided, and with details of what to bring and when to rsvp (soon!).

I learned that this was one reason new arrivals would say it was hard to get to know Danes and get into their social circles. Spontaneity was almost impossible with this level of meticulous forward planning. And most Danes had groups of friends that they kept for life, starting with school, then university.

With our years of arrivals and departures behind us, I had learned that there was only so much energy I could put into getting to know people locally. From my experience in Scotland, where I'd scared new acquaintances with my intense need to get to know them and make friends, I knew that doing the same thing, but in a different language, only to leave again and not keep in touch, would be exhausting. And from a 'local' point of view, there might be resistance to investing in friendship with someone who wasn't sticking around, making the process even more demanding.

So by now I was comfortable with the idea that the mainstay of my social life was the international community. Making local friends was a rewarding bonus, brought deeper connection to the culture, but wasn't always the best use of my energy. I let go of any shame or guilt over not seeking out those relationships. An actual invitation though, where the locals were seeking out our company was an opportunity I seized upon. I replied, put the date in my diary (well, a tiny note on the page of dates for the following year) and proudly displayed the invitation on the fridge.

The next year, we returned from our summer holiday, the kids went back to school, and up popped the reminder: the street party. By now I had learned that this was a fairly traditional event in Danish neighbourhoods, so I was even more determined to take part, learn about the culture, show willing and get to know the faces I occasionally saw in the street. It had also become clear that one reason these events were so well organised was because, for much of the year, even these neighbours who lived beside each other for many years might not talk to each other all that often.

As for my cultural expectations – well, this was a street party, an outdoor event. Although it was in one person's garden, it was clearly a communal, casual get-together. There had been something on the invitation about bringing meat to grill. So it was a barbecue – simple enough! Bring the meat, take a turn cooking it, pass around beers or prosecco from our cooler, chat, get to know some folks, and see how long we last. Right?

Michael was more cynical. We were both introverts, but my brand of introversion came with a love for meeting new people as long as I could recover afterwards. He was happy with who he knew already. He did not want to be dragged along, make small talk, and have to reveal his lack of Danish to our neighbours. Which was definitely reasonable, but I persuaded him to come along, at least for a while. What was the worst that could happen? If the moment came when we weren't enjoying it, we could put down our beers and drift off, claiming another invitation with friends, or a video call with the family back home. He devised his exit strategy carefully.

We filled the cooler with beers and burgers, stepped into the street, and walked the fifty metres to our neighbour across the road.

I groaned inwardly. The first thing I saw on the large driveway was a table set with places for a sit-down meal. This would be no casual hang-out-and-mingle situation.

Michael glared at me.

'Okay, that's not what I was expecting,' I said. 'But it'll be fine!' I forced a smile.

Noise drifted from the garden at the back, so we went round the side of the house. We were on time – we knew enough now about Danish culture not to be late. It must have been one minute past the appointed time. We were the last to arrive.

We were formally welcomed by the host, whom we'd said hello to on the street a couple of times, and he introduced us to everyone else – all middle-aged couples. No children. There were several other young families living on our street. It hadn't occurred to me for a moment that other Danish families wouldn't show up with their kids. I had assumed it was something the whole neighbourhood would take part in.

As we said hello to everyone, I could instantly tell who would be the ones to make the effort to either speak English or patiently engage in a slow and simplified Danish conversation, and which ones would use 'not Danish' as a reason to keep to the easy familiarity of their Dansk-speaking friends.

Then I stood there, waiting for what I assumed would come next. (Why was I still making assumptions about this event?) But no, nobody told me to set our food down by the barbecue, or take it into the kitchen, or that we could add our beers to the cooler, or that we should help ourselves to the drinks from the cooler, or to make ourselves at home, at all.

After an excruciatingly long moment of awkward, silent, smiling eye contact, I said, 'Shall I...?' and lifted my bag of food.

They kept smiling and waited for me to finish my sentence.

'Should I put this over by the barbecue?'

'Oh, you brought food?' said the host.

The invitation had definitely said to bring food.

'That should go in the kitchen then,' he said.

In the kitchen, the hostess eyed me with suspicion. 'Oh, you brought food? Well, I don't know if there's room for it in the fridge.' She sighed as she made a Tetris-like attempt to make space for our burgers and Michael's marinated steaks. Like good Scottish guests, we had brought a bottle of whisky too, which I placed on a sideboard along with drinks for the kids (they would just have to cope with unchilled beverages). At the whisky, her eyes lit up and my kitchen invasion was forgiven.

Back outside, I met Michael's eyes, which were not lit up. His glare had hardened in a way that said, 'Look what else you made me do.'

It turned out there would be games, and we had each been allocated to teams. Michael and Cameron were in one team, Ben and I in another. There was a meticulous plan for the next hour: each team of four would follow an itinerary round a circuit of games set up in several nearby gardens. There was a scoring system. There were rules to follow. We were locked in.

As the afternoon gave way to evening, after learning and forgetting the rules for a boggling variety of Danish garden games, Michael felt he had paid his dues. The excuse of 'the kids are tired' was readily accepted (apparently these parents-of-grown-ups had forgotten the energy potential of a six-year-old) and I was left to navigate the rest of the party on my own.

After another drink in the garden while food was barbecuing, we sat at the table – there were even place cards. Then, another game. Someone handed everyone a slip of paper, and I followed suit as the neighbours each looked at theirs secretively. Someone translated for me: 'This is your challenge during the meal! You have to do what it says on the paper, without telling anyone your secret!' Everyone was very pleased with this idea.

My paper said, 'Tell the person on your left they have great hair.' My heart sank as I stole another glance at my dinner companion, my sixty-ish-year-old host, one of the friendliest in the group but still, someone I had made polite small talk with maybe twice in my life before today. Well, at least he *had* hair.

As the meal went on, multiple courses coming and going, beers draining, conversation becoming louder and livelier, it became clear that these people weren't just neighbours. All the couples at the street party had been in their houses since they were built fifteen years earlier. They had known each other since they bought the land and committed to a building contract. So these couples were rooted in with the houses and knew each other's histories intimately. They were all good friends with our landlord, who had also lived there for the first few years after he had it built. Their children had all grown up and gone to school together. Even if they hadn't been speaking Danish, it would have been almost impossible for me to keep up with the in-jokes and shared memories. Our host sitting next to me did his patient best to keep me clued in. I smiled in surprise or interest, but really, it was all meaningless to me.

Between courses, he and I were chatting about his career. He mentioned he had retired at sixty, several years before.

I was genuinely surprised, and then suddenly realised here was my chance. 'Oh, really? I didn't think you were much over sixty,' I said.

'Is that so?'

'You really don't look it,' I said, and felt myself turning pre-emptively scarlet. 'I mean, your hair is so thick! It looks great.'

He turned to me, eyes wide. 'Um, my goodness. Thank you!'

I couldn't take it any longer. I had to break the rules. 'It was on my paper to compliment your hair.'

'Ah...' he nodded in understanding. 'That makes more sense.'

I squirmed. 'But you do have good hair anyway, I mean, I didn't have to make it up...'

Rescue came when someone stood up and tapped their glass. It was time for speeches. A bottle of schnapps appeared on the table.

By the time almost everyone sitting at the table had made a speech – getting increasingly emotional since one couple was about to move out of the street – another hour had passed. With every toast, there was another shot of schnapps, accompanied each time by progressively sloshier declarations of 'Skål!'. I sneak-ily alternated shots with sips of wine instead.

Finally, the meal was over and I found a reasonably polite moment to make my excuses. 'I better get back and see how the family is getting on.'

But the evening was far from over. 'Tell your husband to come back! He can have some schnapps with us!'

'I'll let him know,' I called over my shoulder as I made my way across the street to safe familiarity. 'Thank you for having us!'

And I *was* grateful. They had welcomed us in with no awareness that every behaviour and tradition was anything other than normal, no awareness of how very Danish they were being. They had no idea that I had crossed the road with a cooler full of assumptions and expectations they couldn't possibly meet. It wasn't just because of their Danishness. Friends in other neighbourhoods had talked about street parties that were more the casual barbecue I'd envisaged, with plenty of young children joining in.

Here I'd encountered another layer of culture: the culture of this street. Did they even know their way of doing things differed from two suburbs over? As I walked past houses where young children lived, cars absent from the driveways, I wondered if those Danes had moved into the neighbourhood and experienced the same culture shock as me when they showed up for their first street party – just without the added foreignness that I had brought. It reminded me of moments in childhood when I got invited to a friend's house for tea – not dinner? – and the food was on trays, not the table, or the juice was a different flavour, or ITV instead of BBC was on in the background. Those were moments of discovering that our family life – our family culture – was distinct to us, not a default normality. I'd gone through that repeatedly as an expat, discovering that what I'd assumed was normal was just weird, quirky Britishness.

I still carried those assumptions around with me, still had to process the cognitive load of daily unfamiliarity. I was grateful to arrive at our own driveway – the refuge of our familiar family culture.

THE NEWSPAPER

On a dark Danish November evening in 2019 – into our second year in Denmark – I proudly slapped a pile of newspapers on the edge of a rehearsal room stage. I watched my new friends each grab a copy and flick through it, scanning the pages.

'It's on page nineteen!' I said, watching eagerly.

This story had begun on the train to Odense, earlier in the year. That wintry February morning, I dropped the kids at school and took the car to Michael's office by the harbour so he could pick them up later. I walked from the harbour to the town, catching beautiful snowy views of Esbjerg on the way. I installed myself at my usual table in Espresso House for a while, then joined the Danish class.

When a friend asked me to go for lunch after, I had a quick response. 'No, can't do that I'm afraid. I'm off to catch the train to Odense!'

Denmark's third-largest city, the birthplace of Hans Christian Andersen, was only ninety minutes away, but where we were, tucked away on the west coast, taking the trip to the bigger city felt like an adventure.

'What? Why? What about the children?'

I bit my tongue, resisting the urge for a snarky comment about them having a whole other parent.

'Oh, that's fine, Michael is picking them up today.'

'And he doesn't mind?'

I ignored that one. 'I'm going to an event for *The International.* Have you heard of it?'

At that time, the magazine for internationals living in Denmark was not distributed in Esbjerg. I'd found it via social media and was paying close attention. I'd even contacted the editor, Lyndsay, to ask if she needed an Esbjerg writer, and she wanted to keep in touch. So when they announced a series of events to celebrate their first anniversary, I made my way to the nearest one to see who I could meet.

It was my first visit to Odense, and the event was late in the afternoon, so I planned to explore the city, have some solo lunch, and shop in the Danish department store Magasin, which didn't have a branch in Esbjerg.

After I got off the train, I sought out the bar where the event would take place, then passed a happy couple of hours in solo exploration of Odense's pretty centre. In the mood for a new outfit, I bought a sparkly jumper. The sparkles felt important.

Despite other people's surprise when I said I was going to another city, on my own, to an event where I knew no one, I wasn't nervous. I was excited. What was the worst that could happen? If I felt completely out of place, I would go back to the train after one drink, having visited somewhere new, and I would at least have a physical copy of the paper in my hands. More likely: I would meet some interesting people, make small talk, and learn a bit more about *The International*. Best case: I'd become part of a community of internationals and writers, and have a new outlet for my writing.

Still, in that worst-case, unlikely-but-possible scenario, a sparkly jumper would definitely help me ride it out with a shine.

I went into a cosy bar just down the road from the venue and had a glass of wine while I waited. About fifteen minutes after the event was due to start, I made my way, fashionably late (these were internationals rather than just Danes, after all), to the bar, and entered through the wide glass doors. I primed myself to scan the room for a face I might recognise from social media, while confidently striding to the bar to order a drink.

To my great relief, before I could even clock who I was looking at, Lyndsay instantly recognised me, and greeted me with a huge smile.

'Hello, Catriona!' she said. 'You came here from Esbjerg! That's so good of you!' Since I'd contacted her, she'd been keeping me in mind for when she could free up more pages in the monthly publication.

'I can't believe you came all this way!' she continued. In a small country like Denmark, crossing from one side of Jutland to the other and onto another island represented a substantial commitment. I already knew from her reaction that I had locked in my access to those pages when they came up.

'Come over here and meet Keri. She's a writer for the paper who came with me today from Copenhagen.' And that was when the best-case scenario became even better. I may have spent the first twenty minutes of our friendship completely distracted by how much this woman reminded me of Jennifer Saunders, but she was to become a pivotal person in my writing community. It took a while for Keri and I to reconnect after that first meeting, but as writing buddies we've given each other huge support with our writing projects.

I spent the rest of the event meeting Odense-based internationals, politely explaining to each of them the answer to 'How long have you lived in Odense?' Those conversations were full of potential connections and projects that I knew I would most likely never act on, but I boarded the train back to Esbjerg energised beyond the buzz from the couple of beers I'd had. It confirmed for me this lesson: there was always room for more. Sure, I wasn't about to commute to be part of the international community in Odense, but at that event I sparked one genuine friendship, and met up with people whose journeys I continued to pay attention to. Who could say when those connections would spark something else?

Just a few weeks later, the editor got back to me with the offer of a monthly column about being an international in Esbjerg, and that became a focus for my writing life.

***

On that November night in the rehearsal room, I was keen to share my latest column with my friends, the other members of a fledgling international theatre group. Our project was the perfect example of the theme I'd written about for that month's article, and I wanted them to celebrate it with me. It was all about how we were '...doing something that's never been done before in Esbjerg; we're blazing a trail, mapping out new territory, pushing through to a new frontier.' I captured the idea of Esbjerg as a young town in the 'wild-ish' west of Denmark, where it was easy to bring into existence whatever the town didn't have already, to do it by your own rules. 'Meanwhile, in that hall in Huset, full of buzzing youthful energy, my new friends and I have found each other in our niche, are taking a chance, and forging something new.'

When I first showed up to join the group earlier that year, instead of a sparkly top to help give me confidence, this time I had the armour of my biker-style leather jacket to help bring me forth into a room full of strangers.

As we came to the end of our first year in Esbjerg, I knew I needed theatre back in my life. I'd been looking out for options – among all the evening classes and clubs that the Danes loved, there were several options, but all in Danish. My comfortable level with that language was still ordering pastries. When someone else posted in the international Facebook group looking for the same thing, I promptly replied, 'I haven't found one, but let me know if you decide to start something!' hoping to seed the idea and avoid taking the initiative.

Sure enough, by late spring the same person posted she was going to gather anyone interested in an English-language theatre group, and I got myself into that message thread.

Valentina and her friend Juan Carlos, who'd also encouraged her to take the initiative, were both international masters students, and the group started meeting over the summer, while I was on holiday. So it was late August before I could show up. They met in a community cultural centre called 'Huset' ('the house') in the middle of town. I knew it housed an independent cinema, and a cosy-looking bar, but it was volunteer-run and I'd only ever seen it being used for specific kommune or student events as I walked past it on my way in and out of the library.

On the balmy summer evening, I parked in the large car park beside the building and made my way towards the entrance. I had no idea what this group would be like, had met none of them; I didn't know what their plans were, and they were clearly all a good bit younger than me. I told myself I was just checking things out; there was no need to commit to anything at this stage. Hopeful as I was, it all seemed quite precarious, but I would be bitterly disappointed if I didn't feel at least a glimmer of belonging on this Monday night, with two years in Esbjerg still ahead. I approached a group of folk lingering in the little garden out front. 'Um...is this the theatre group? Are we waiting here?'

'Yes, yes,' said a man in his late twenties with a strong Hispanic accent. 'We are just waiting for someone to arrive with the key.'

Moments later, I was following the small group upstairs and into a hall. Our volunteer member with the key, Tuan, went to a complicated-looking electrical board, and flipped a series of switches which I would never learn, and there, lit up before me, was a world of possibility: a long hall with a wooden floor, taking up half the first floor of the building. Best of all, there was a large stage at the far end, fully equipped with lights and drapes, a black blank canvas. Tuan lifted the flap hanging from the front of the stage to haul out a truck full of chairs, and we set ourselves up in a circle for the first of many, many sessions of introductions and ice-breakers.

Two hours later, I went back down the stairs, waving a cheery 'I lige måde!' (same to you) to the volunteers now on duty for the film session that night who'd wished us a good evening. I was confident in new friendships and buzzing with the energy of connection. Not everyone who was there that night remained part of the team, but I knew I already had new friends.

Back in the hall three months later, showing off my light-hearted six hundred words, with my writer bio at the side, to my friends who shared very few of my circumstances but absolutely shared my need for this project, I knew I had found a sense of home in myself that I would carry with me wherever we landed.

It had taken a determined and even rebellious spirit to keep focused on this outlet for creativity and identity and deep connection that went beyond small talk over coffee with large groups of new people.

From my international theatre groups, book groups I'd joined and started, and other projects like conversation groups, I'd learned how important it was for me to connect with people for a reason, for a purpose, over and above the connection that comes from circumstance. I had important friendships with other expat spouses, neighbours, parents of my kids' friends, people who were with the same company, came from the same place, and speak the same language. Having those experiences in common led to strong connections. But my circumstances were not the same as who I was at my core.

The friendships I made with people because we connected over performance, or books, or because we worked on a passion project together, those were important in a different way. They connected with a deeper, stronger part of my identity, one that was a constant, regardless of circumstance. They connected with the sense of myself that made me feel at home wherever I was.

Why did that feel rebellious? Because often how I chose to spend my time – whether working for myself, creating a portable career outside of employment, or in a hobby that took me out of the conventional social sphere of the playground mum, the wife, the company, the coffee mornings and cookie decorating classes – that surprised people. Sometimes I could see an unspoken reaction: *We can do that?* After I arrived in Kampala with a baby and a toddler, and with all the culture shock of motherhood and family separation on top of the physical move, I would have been surprised too. When I had time for myself, I spent it studying TEFL, not knowing I could step off the 'teacher' track I had been on for years. I did my best to fit in with spouse events and being the lady of the house, did my best to be a good expat. When I finally answered that call to show up for an audition, it got me back on a track to somewhere I belonged.

It felt ridiculous to think of connecting to that deeper sense of self as a rebellion. But the cultural pull I had felt (as a woman) to fulfil a role in a certain, very visible way was powerful and compelling. In the world of expat families, where despite all our awareness of gender stereotyping and bias, the traditional gender divide was still prevalent, the alternative became almost invisible.

THE BEACH

The beach was my retreat – the beach in winter, at least. On the mornings when I needed to get out of the hobbithole and have an outlook on the rest of the world, I would drive ten minutes west and park next to Esbjerg's iconic sculpture, *Mennesket ved Havet* (Man Meets the Sea): four giant seated human figures of white stone facing the part of the North Sea called the Wadden Sea.

In the car, I would still have that foggy feeling, the feeling of having had to get up in the dark, in a closed-up, too-warm house, of being not quite ready for the day, and being weighed down by too many woolly layers.

But walking onto the sand, the perspective was boundless. I immersed myself in the fresher-than-fresh cold sea air as it washed away my grumpy morning mood. The juxtaposition of the industrial harbour's dramatic skyline with the natural haven of the Wadden Sea and the beach invigorated me. Plovers along the shoreline had their own industrious concerns, pecking for shellfish at the water's edge. They would scurry away to pick off another stretch as I got closer. I relished being at the edge of the land, open to the elements.

As autumn became the dark, oppressive November of our second Danish winter, I needed those beach moments more often than before. They became my morning medication, the vitamin sea that injected extra serotonin into my days. I had slowly become aware that I was sinking into a depression, and I was trying to manage it. At least I knew this for what it was – knowledge that was the silver lining of having had depression before.

Back in my late twenties, I'd learned a lot about the power of negative thinking, and how to reframe those thoughts to gain perspective. Coming out of that period, I could look back and see there were habits and behaviours to avoid. I knew it was not just antidepressants that had helped me through, but also the small acts of attention to myself that had begun with finally recognising that how I felt wasn't normal.

When I was depressed in Uganda, I'd had to untangle and unravel the impact of relentless transition with hormonal changes on my body, and the very real effects of culture shock.

But here in Denmark, life was steadier. We had routine and predictability (for now, at least) and I loved the lifestyle. I was pursuing my own ambitions with a genuine sense of purpose, and I had reconnected to deeper parts of myself with creative pursuits and by actively seeking a deep sense of community. Nothing was wrong, nothing was bad. I was happy.

That's how I knew I was depressed.

Despite being happy, I had stopped enjoying any of the things that made me happy. There was no transition or disruption or overwhelming challenge in my life to point to. But the bad days were no longer just aligned with my cycle. There were way more bad days than good ones. I knew I needed to give my body the movement and light and clarity to hold on to a perspective based on reality, to regain my core functioning self. Some days, that started at the beach.

I couldn't see the bad days coming, though. Sometimes I would wake up and get on with my day before it hit me.

At the time, I was writing with focus, pulling together words. And so, when one of the bad days hit hard, that was where I focused the words.

***

My plan for the day was to work out of the house. I'd built up a bit of a habit of starting the day in Espresso House over a long coffee, then when that burst of inspiration slowed down, I'd move on to the library or another café. I was determined to follow my plan, so I'd been ready for the day before the school run, my laptop in my bag. With no opportunity to hesitate, I headed straight for my parking spot overlooking the harbour, and soon I was at my favourite table, with my favourite Ethiopian brew at my side.

I opened the file where my book – this book – was in progress. I had signed up for National Novel Writing Month (NaNoWriMo) – a commitment to write fifty thousand words in November, so although there was a plan of sorts, I didn't always follow it in the push to get as many words down as possible. I'd write memories from Uganda, or Pau, or the day before: wherever the words took me. There was always something relevant floating around.

But this time there was nothing – no focus at all. A heavy feeling descended, seemingly from nowhere. Every time, it brought just a little more grace to accept it and forgive it. But there it was: 'Oh, I'm sad now. There's nothing good in here, around me.' I kept the laptop open while I finished my coffee, performing busy-ness. Not that there were many others around to pay any attention. But I moved my mouse around, opened some windows and closed them again. Wrote a word, deleted it, wrote two more, deleted.

I was shell-less. Soft and susceptible. A mollusc. I wondered if this was a familiar feeling to all but the most zealous of morning people – that moment before fully waking up, when there's no capacity to concentrate on any decisions. But with face washed, coffee drunk, and fully dressed, the shell is intact – armour against the day.

On my bad days, the shell was never there, there was no capacity to focus or concentrate on anything other than keeping it together, appearing normal. All my mental energy went to not-crying, not yet. The edge was precarious; I could fall over it at any given moment, at the slightest disturbance.

I decided to take practical steps. I packed up my laptop and made my way along the pedestrianised street under a grey Danish autumn sky, a bitter wind penetrating my biker jacket, the armour that wasn't doing its job today. I couldn't walk past Normal, the Danish drugstore chain that always stocks random imports from other countries, without checking for something familiar. I was in luck – there was Cadbury's chocolate. Not the focus of my mission, but a little source of pleasure for my arsenal.

At the pharmacy, I asked for Rescue Remedy, hoping for a little herbal help in quelling the anxiety that was eating away at my concentration. I hadn't gone looking for it in Denmark before, and I had left my bottle of it at home that day. The very enthusiastic assistant was keen to reassure me that yes, he could speak English with me, or German if I preferred. He'd never heard of it, but urged me to explain it to him, so that maybe he could find a Danish version. I demurred, and said I was also looking for a cough mixture, and approximately eight questions later he had found out exactly what kind of cough mixture I wanted. I tried to smile, but I resented the extra effort it took to validate his eager language practice.

I found a Rescue Remedy spray at the cosmetics chain Matas. After the prescribed number of puffs, and an extra one for good measure, I crossed the main square towards the library. I knew the walk would do me good, the change of scene would be important. If I could get myself sitting somewhere where I could start typing words, where they would flow and I could stop myself from thinking about every other tiny thing, then I could feel productive, and get the sense of accomplishment that was a reliable antidote to how I was feeling.

I briefly congratulated myself with a mental pat on the back. 'See? You're doing the right things! You know what to do.'

I passed the barber where we took the boys. I remembered how badly they needed haircuts, and how I had to fit that in soon, and how even Cameron had been complaining about the tufts of hair at the back of his neck. Responsibility suddenly piled in on me. It all felt impossible. I felt something crumble inside; I was welling up, right there in the middle of the town.

I turned around. To head back…where? To go back to the car and go home.

But we needed groceries.

I would drive to the supermarket on the way, tick off the shopping list, and at least that would be done. An accomplishment.

Other than that: no productivity for today. I was giving in.

Making my way back across the square, I darted my gaze from person to person, between boxy buildings, from one shop window to another. I couldn't ignore any of it, couldn't shut down my perceptions and reactions to every detail.

The bright flashy banner pasted across a shop window declaring promotional discounts felt like an attack, its Danish words hostile to my reason. Usually the word 'Slutspurt' – such an unfortunate combination of syllables for the anglophone – made me laugh, but this time I felt bullied. I wanted to shut it out, but I couldn't.

On these bad days, that was what the depression did. Everything around me only existed in its otherness. I only saw how people were not like me, or would not like me. Everything was opposition, complications, barriers or hurdles. It was like a cognitive filter on the world, blocking out the light rays on what I can relate to, blocking out comfort, or touchstones, or perspective.

I couldn't be happy today – but I could be organised, I could get the shopping done.

On the way back to the car, a jumble of thoughts about my writing goal took over. I needed three thousand words to stay on track for the day. But, I told myself, it was okay for life to get in the way of work. I couldn't control being ill or depressed. I could let myself off. Then I thought that today was just one day, and in five days it would be the end of NaNoWriMo, and even if all the other days I could write the words, maybe I wouldn't finish without today's words, and wouldn't that be even more depressing to get so close to winning and not succeed.

I decided to get in the car and have a cry. That was the next weapon. Cry it out of my system, let my body flush out the toxic emotions. Then I would drive to the library car park. If there was a space, I would work there; if there were no spaces, I would drive to the supermarket instead. It felt comforting to let fate decide.

But before I could even get in the car, I noticed another car entering the small, sought-after location, and my heart sank. The driver would see me getting in my car and wait for me to drive off to get my space.

The crying would have to wait.

I drove to the library with the latest episode of one of my favourite writing podcasts playing. Listening to other voices was better than letting my own thoughts run rampant and reckless. These were the best kind of voices, generous writers talking about how they conveyed themselves on the page, how they got the words done and how they discovered even themselves as they write.

It was helping.

Amazingly, there were several spaces in the library car park. I took one, switched off the engine, and finished listening to the podcast, because it was so miraculously relevant. This writer was talking about the story she wrote about herself, and about how the tiny details were very important. I finished listening, took myself into the library, and wrote down every tiny detail of the day.

The Doctor

B ecause I knew that I was happy and also depressed, it was time to get medical help. It was clear there was something chemical going on, and I knew hormones were playing their part too; my cycle was short – just three weeks, with several days of draining mood swings.

Although we were automatically registered with a local doctor in Esbjerg, so far I'd only taken the kids to appointments. I prepared myself for my first visit to a Danish doctor.

At least I didn't have to phone to make the appointment. There was no real language barrier verbally in Denmark, because most of the population spoke English fluently. But I hated that moment of asking someone to speak English, especially on the phone, when my attempt at the Danish pronunciation of 'Er det ok hvis jeg taler Engelsk?' would throw them off and I'd have to repeat it in English anyway. 'Is it okay if I speak English?' At times, it felt too vulnerable to have to rely on someone being helpful just to communicate.

But Danish society was one of the most digitalised in Europe, so I could make the appointment online. Because it was my first time, I could still choose which doctor to go to. There were two women on the practice website, and I picked the older of them, the one more likely to have empathy for ongoing mental health and hormonal issues, or at least more experience of it in their patients.

When the day of my appointment arrived, it felt like a Good Day. But I wasn't sure if that was a Good Thing. On a good day, I would present as being fully in possession of perspective, as being confident and resilient, and I'd have to fight the instinct to play down my concerns. I wasn't looking for this doctor to see me and instantly reach for her prescription pad. I would have been worried if she had. But I wanted to be taken seriously, and I wanted to take myself seriously. Trying to convey the hair-trigger that lay between, 'I can communicate my health needs concisely and be treated like an adult,' and 'But from one day to another I can find myself on the edge of an abyss and I become a barely functioning amoeba so I actually need some help,' felt like an impossible task.

In anticipation of both possibilities – either not looking like someone struggling with depression, or being tearful and unable to communicate – I had spent a lot of time writing down the details of my history with mental health and hormones, so that I could summarise them as quickly as possible but still be taken seriously. Denmark has a publicly funded health system like the UK's NHS, so I knew the appointment would be short.

So I had notes.

I kept them to one page of a pocket-sized notebook: one small piece of paper to summarise the mental health history of a forty-five-year-old woman over several countries, and to explain concisely what I was feeling, and what I understood it to be. I kept the language as simple as possible, not certain of the doctor's level of English. I didn't know whether she would be like the family doctor I'd seen at twenty-nine, who knew me, knew the family history, and was a lifelong advocate for women's health, or whether she'd be a no-nonsense, it's-all-in-your-head type, or just someone who'd never really experienced mental health problems, and who would struggle to empathise no matter how hard she tried.

I had a conversation in Congo once with a friend whose daughter was experiencing depression. She found it so hard to understand because, she said, 'I just always wake up happy.' It blew my mind that someone would experience the world that way, just as it bewildered her, I'm sure, to discover how many people around her understood what her daughter was going through.

***

The doctor's surgery was always efficient. I simply had to scan my yellow card, with the CPR number that afforded access to all Danish public services, to check in for my appointment. I sat opposite the waiting room fish tank, clutching my little notebook, flipping the cover open again and again to check my notes, breathing slowly out through my mouth, trying to trust myself to navigate the next five minutes without either falling apart or backtracking over the whole thing.

The handle turned on the door to the consultation rooms. I concentrated my attention on it, ready to listen out for whatever unexpected pronunciation of my name I might hear.

It was my turn, and I followed the middle-aged woman with dark brown hair back to her consultation room. I asked if we could speak English; of course she said yes.

As we got the brief small talk out of the way – I'm Scottish, I've lived here for just over a year, yes I like it fine – I realised her own accent wasn't Danish. She had moved here from eastern Europe some years before. Okay then, she would get it. This was going to be fine.

She asked the question.

'Well,' I said, 'I'm here for my mental health. I'm depressed.' And before she could ask me anything else, I worked my way through my notes as clearly and efficiently as I could. I did my best to summarise it all, this lifetime of insight gained into my complex self and what I needed. I did my best to make it succinct, clear, and understandable – a challenge for someone who comes from a culture where we still sometimes lack the language for that. And just because I knew it deep in my body, didn't mean it could be easily translated into words. But I did it, for myself, and for this stranger, who didn't know one thing about me, or my culture, or my lifestyle.

I told her about my first clinical depression diagnosis in my late twenties, following various attempts to manage PMT; through pregnancies and breast-feeding in my thirties I'd continued seeking help with my hormones and mood swings; I'd had counselling in Uganda; today, I was suffering with a short cycle and more moods swings, effectively spending a third of my life in thrall to those hormones, feeling my resilience weaken every time. I added this: that a decade of globally mobile life had taught me I needed not just resilience, but super-resilience, to thrive. Finally I said, 'Life here is good. I'm contented and happy. I love our lifestyle, and I do thrive in it. But I know I'm depressed because I can't find daily joy in any of it. My experiences have taught me that this is depression, that this is what it looks like even when life is good.'

I flipped the notebook closed.

She paused, put down her pen, thought for a moment.

She said, 'Can't you just go home?'

She didn't get it at all.

Then she said, 'You need to think positive.'

I wanted to shout back at her all the things that I did shout at the car steering wheel ten minutes later. 'You haven't heard a word I said! This has got nothing to do with circumstances! I don't want to go home, I like it here! Did you think that a woman like me, with my life experience, who very rarely seeks medical help, would pack up her whole mental health history for a stranger, in a foreign language, in a foreign country with an unfamiliar medical system, just to be told to think positive?'

Of course, the doctor knew nothing about what kind of woman I was, and a medical practitioner with a brand new patient has to start from the beginning.

But I was so much further ahead than the beginning.

So much for my Good Day. But it was tears of frustration in the car on the way home that day, tears of righteous anger, rather than internal collapse. Truthfully, I knew I was already on the road to recovery just from having made the appointment, and saying out loud that I needed help. If the doctor wouldn't give it, I was at least now ready to gather up other resources and strategies I had relied on in the past.

There was one positive outcome. She gave me the referral I needed for a gynaecologist, since my birth control was due for review, anyway. I was sure a hormonal adjustment would help.

So a couple of weeks later, I disrobed in a cubicle with a sign that said, 'I bought this sign to remind you of how beautiful you look when you smile.' The gynaecologist (also not Danish) listened to me describe my cycle. Her reaction brought instant relief, and was what I needed to hear: 'Oh, that is no good at all! We can definitely do something about that!'

Even before she had booked me in for the follow-up, and sent me away with a list of herbal supplements she was sure would help me, I already felt better, knowing that I'd been seen and heard, and that I'd been trusted to know myself.

I'd gone too long without that recognition that there was a better way. There it was: the paradox of being a serial expat, of successfully navigating transition over and over again. I got better at it. I learned how to handle it. And when we get better at something, we stop seeing that it's still hard, that it's a difficult thing to do. We forget that we still need that super-resilience, because we are coping, we are capable. We look and present as being incredibly capable because we are doing very hard things, things that lots of people wouldn't even contemplate.

So we forget to use some of that strength and resilience to shore us up for the next time. That we can seek support, that there are ways to make it easier, even as these are the challenges we've chosen, and it's the lifestyle we relish.

I had learned to be at home in my identity, and in my purpose, and with the work that I was doing in Denmark. Maybe I still had a lot to learn about being at home in my body.

Then again, everything I thought I had learned about feeling at home wherever I was in the world was about to be turned upside down.

THE TRAMPOLINE

It was a Thursday morning. A stranger knocked at our door. A surprising and unusual thing for a Danish suburb at the best of times, in a country where people leave each other to their privacy. But on this particular day it was not just unusual, it was unnerving, alarming.

Frowning, I opened the door and stood well back. The woman on my doorstep also stepped back several paces.

'Hej,' she began, 'Jeg er –'

'Undskyld...taler du engelsk?' As I asked her to speak English, a cold sweat crept up my spine.

'Oh, yes. I am your neighbour from behind. Your trampoline is blowing away. It is on top of our hedge.'

My shoulders fell with relief that she wasn't delivering worse news. I thanked her for letting me know as she backed further away then headed home. But my stomach was broiling with anxiety at the impossibility of it all.

I was still in pyjamas, so I quickly threw on jeans and boots, left the boys on the sofa with their bonus TV time, and ventured to the garden at the back of the house, through the hurricane winds that had descended that morning, like the raven himself.

Sure enough, our large trampoline had upended itself on top of the two-metre-high hedge separating our two gardens. We'd installed it with the strongest anchoring system we could find, knowing already the stories of other trampolines taking flight with the west coast winds. It had held fast through previous storms, but this morning, the elements were having their way. The strong winds tugged on it, buffeting the nets and pulling at the flat surface. Although for the moment it was tangled in the hedge, there was no knowing when a stronger gust would grab it free and send it flying further towards someone's roof – or worse, someone's head.

Michael was at his office, setting things in order, gathering what he would need for the weeks ahead. There was no option this morning to call on friends to come over and help. I was on my own. There was nothing else for it but to pull down the trampoline and dismantle it myself. I didn't want the boys to help, because I was sure that I was risking injury from a gust catching a stray branch or bungee cord at any moment.

For two hours, I battled with the nets, elastic cords, and rusted screws that held the trampoline together. Having tugged, pulled, and attempted some un-tangling, I had to conclude it was too completely caught on the hedge for me to get it onto the ground. I would have to dismantle it in position: upside down at a forty-degree angle, mostly two metres in the air. Even with the help of a ladder, I couldn't reach well enough to undo some attachments.

With the gusts whipping at my tears, my only option was to sacrifice the trampoline in the name of neighbourhood safety. The Stanley knife was my friend as I hacked at cords to detach the dangerous sail of the trampoline's surface. My screams of frustration were lost in the wind, a torrent of sharp words adding to the sharp tools I used to slash at something my boys loved. The fun was being ripped away.

It all felt pretty apocalyptic.

The night before, Wednesday March 11 2020, at around nine p.m., Michael and I were in a non-Danish bubble. We had never connected Danish TV in our house – the age of Netflix and other streaming services was an entertainment blessing and an integration curse. We were happily watching an episode of *Curb Your Enthusiasm* when my phone started pinging furiously in the corner where it was charging. I tried to leave it alone later in the evenings, to focus on just one thing, even if it was the screen of the television. So I ignored the alerts for a while, sure that someone was sharing random updates in a class parents Whatsapp chat. As the credits rolled on an episode, Michael reached for his phone. He raised his eyebrows, looked at me, and told me the news: 'All Danish schools are closing from Monday, with kids to be kept home from tomorrow for anyone who is able. And everyone is to work from home if they can.'

For a long moment, I just gazed back at him, speechless, as my skin prickled from the flood of nervous adrenaline in my system. Eventually, 'So that's why my phone is making such a racket then,' I weakly suggested.

So, it was real. It was serious. At nine p.m. Mette Frederiksen, the Danish Prime Minister, gave a press conference announcing measures to combat the spread of COVID-19. Although it was a sudden move, there had already been some scaling back of big events in Denmark, and the drastic situation in Italy was dominating headlines.

Michael was sporting his best regretful I-told-you-so face. He'd been asking me to add extra supplies to our shopping for weeks, since about mid-January, when lockdown began in parts of China. I did it to humour him, really, with the phrase 'pick your battles' in mind, knowing his natural tendency towards pessimism, and knowing that his thought process always ticked over to the worst-case scenario. I chose buying unnecessary canned goods, filling up the freezer, buying extra bags of pasta, and finding storage space for it all, over getting into arguments and adding to his anxiety. I sucked up the discomfort of feeling self-conscious in the hardware store, where I filled my trolley with candles, water purifiers, and wind-up flashlights. By that time, yes, Italy was deep in the crisis, and Denmark had a handful of cases, but I had to point out to him that even in China, no one had ever lost power, that Italians could still shop for food (reassuring myself, as much as anything). Still, he said, 'Humour me,' and I did.

The day before the announcement of Denmark's lockdown measures, I had gone to a branch of a supermarket I didn't normally use in search of long-life UHT milk. I bumped into another international friend on the way in, and in our inevitable chat about supermarket choices, I mentioned what I was hoping to find. 'Oh, I don't know if they have that here,' she said, then frowned at me, 'but you're not panic-buying are you?'

'Well, no...' I said, 'but...stocking up a bit, just in case.'

'The Danes will never do that. They trust their government too much.'

I only added four extra litres of the UHT milk to my basket, but I detected some dirty looks from fellow shoppers, sure enough, although perhaps I imagined it.

That night, after the announcement, Michael felt vindicated, and I felt relieved, as we saw in our social feeds that Copenhagen supermarket shelves were being cleared within an hour of the announcement. I felt that rare, for me, but recognisable gnawing feeling in the bottom of my gut, as anxiety and uncertainty took over, and my mind created scenes of disorder and scarcity.

Still tapping away at his phone, Michael said, 'We should go home before they close the borders.' He searched for flights.

He said we should go back.

And every fibre of my being cried out against it.

I picked this battle.

I said no.

I was already home.

***

I had always said I would go back.

In the early months in Pau, I would talk about going home again in the future. Then I would bristle inwardly at the comments from 'helpful' people who would smile knowingly, condescendingly it seemed, and say, 'Oh, you can't go back. Give it five years, and you'll never be able to go back.' I was both resentful of their assumption and terrified that they might be right.

For the first thirty-five years of my life, I was rooted in the place I came from and the place where I chose to live. I had spent more than a decade of my adult life building a career, a life, an identity in one city, Aberdeen, built from solid granite. I didn't just belong to those streets; they belonged to me. My identity was rooted in a sense of a city, and of a country.

So when people told me I would change too much to still be that person, it raised my defences; I would not countenance such a thing. It meant that to begin with, I protested too much, held on to that idea of myself and my sense of home so much that I held at bay other places and other possibilities. Over the years I'd learned, not to let go of the roots, there were still roots there, but to add more branches, put down more roots. Along the way I'd realised that 'roots' is plural, after all. Taking root somewhere wasn't a zero-sum game – it didn't preclude more roots branching out into other places. My roots could spread, deeper in some places, shallower in others, taking up what they need from each rich source.

But still, I planned to go back. The truth of having had that sense of place to begin with was such an important part of me I couldn't imagine not giving my children an opportunity to experience it. I knew we wouldn't return to the same version of my life, or with the same version of me. But I would return to the idea of continuity, of roots that go deep in one place.

For all the amazing advantages that a serial expat life gave my children – which did outweigh the challenges, or the losses – that continuity was something they inevitably lacked. If they don't live it, they can't miss it, and every globally mobile journey is different. But I missed it *for* them. My experience growing up had that sense of continuity, of, in my case, learning dance skills from the same teachers over ten years of classes, and later, attending drama classes, of finding a second home in our local theatre, of being known there by the same people – as a second generation there, even. I wanted my boys to go 'home' one day, to a home they didn't know yet, to get that opportunity to follow a path with a more certain destination.

And I wanted it for myself, even if I imagined getting itchy feet again later. I wanted to give myself a reprieve from the cycle of perception, evaluation, comparison, that comes with repeated transition and culture shock.

And yet, in a time of crisis?

I didn't go back.

I point blank refused to go back.

***

When Michael instinctively reached for an escape route, he had practical reasons on his side, concerns about citizenship, family, and property. Our only access to the language was my very basic Danish; we still found aspects of the culture bewildering. Leaving when we chose would be preferable to being forced to leave for any reason. In his worst-case scenario mindset, he did not want us to be foreigners when the apocalypse came.

While I felt secure enough to dismiss the idea of being run out of town by rake-wielding Danish suburbanites who would blame us foreigners for their lack of resources, he had a point about taking action while we could keep some control.

Still, no matter what his practical head was telling me, my heart – my whole body – was screaming 'No! We stay!' Through my visceral, emotional haze, I grasped at some practical straws of my own.

With two family members in Scotland squarely in the vulnerable category, we would not be getting off a plane and rushing straight to see them. We'd have to put our housesitter out of our house. The whole idea of getting on a plane, travelling among strangers, and risking exposure felt wrong. Not to mention all that bloody shopping he'd had me do! A task I hated at the best of times, and now every cabinet was stocked; the freezer was full to bursting. He wanted me to go to another country, leave all that behind, and start again?

I knew they were weak arguments.

In so many logistical ways, when we needed a port in a storm, we could have gone 'home', and we would have been in the right place.

I fought back hot tears. How could I explain, how could I rationalise the overwhelming sensation, deep in my core, that we were already in the right place?

Equally visceral was the sense of comfort and relief that I had, sitting on that sofa, in that well-stocked house, as I heard tales of fresh food disappearing from shelves (short-lived though the Danish panic turned out to be). With the news that we wouldn't be able to go anywhere else for the foreseeable future, I already felt comfortable and at ease. We already had everything to hand, to keep us fed, working, and occupied over the weeks to come, all within the walls of our compact, perfectly designed Scandinavian home. By contrast, our Aberdeen house, apart from not being apocalypse-prepped, had never been our home for more than a few weeks at a time – we'd bought it when we lived in Congo. Yes, it would be our forever house, a privileged and valuable base. I loved it, and one day it absolutely would be the place where I would feel comfortable, where I would have ease. But for now, it was a place where we lived out of a suitcase, where we grocery-shopped for the short term, where I could have with me only the things that I had packed for that visit.

Where we were now, there was ease in our routines, the products of hundreds of micro-decisions made over time – albeit a short, intense time – decisions I wouldn't have to make for the foreseeable future: where to shop, what to add to the list, what to cook. The places we could go for bike rides and walks. The regular arrival of the window-cleaner. The simple rhythm to our hours and days at home – a structure that was surely about to become more important than ever. What we did when we woke up, which parts of the house we used. Where we got the dishes from to set the table. The comforting ritual of laundry-folding right at that spot in the laundry room where it's easy, with my encouraging podcast in the background. The pile of books waiting to be read, the stash of craft items to occupy a rainy day. More than ever, I craved the nest I had built around us.

To suddenly pack up and go, and be somewhere without those daily routines and rituals, to start again with all that decision-making...in that moment I could see it all, and how exhausting it would be, even before adding in the big decisions, about schooling, costs, whether to travel around the country to see vulnerable family.

To be sitting on that sofa, and to stay there, and to not have to invest energy in all those decisions – that felt, in a deeply privileged and comforting way, like home.

Then I thought about people.

I thought about my 'Esbjerg Tribe', the friends of less than eighteen months, the ones who were always available, who I'd travelled with, the ones who didn't hold back, because they'd lived in a multitude of countries and cultures, and had that special expat superpower of connecting instantly, of knowing we needed each other from day one. They weren't there two years ago, and in years to come some of them would be distant again. But they were there the day before, and they'd be there the next day. We would only see each other via Whatsapp for a while to come, but somehow, I felt I needed to be near them, just in case. They lived just minutes away and could help in a crisis. And more than that, what I felt more powerfully, was that I could help *them* in a crisis. I thought of Polina, my Bulgarian friend who'd been solo parenting for months while her husband worked in Italy, and now he was stuck there behind closed borders for who-knows-how-long. I thought of friends in families where both parents would have to work from home while homeschooling demanding kids. I thought of the ones who struggled with anxiety, the ones whose culture felt particularly distant from the host Danish culture, the ones whose children were too small to understand, the ones who were still just getting settled in here. Those people, the ones here in this town, were the ones I could be of use to.

They were the third culture friends who felt like home wherever I went.

I felt at home where we had routine, ease, comfort, and our people. I could have that one day in Scotland. But not in a crisis, and not in a hurry.

It was an ironic turn of events.

I had learned over a decade of nomadic living that home could be anywhere I was, anywhere my family was, that it didn't depend on being in one specific place, that it could be many places all at once, that it was layers of places, and pieces of my heart scattered across the globe. That home was where the heart was. That the four walls and the nature of the ground under our feet, whether granite, or red dust, or Pyrenean foothills, or the North Sea coast, or the bustling urban hills of Kampala or the flat, wide suburbs of Jutland, were not the things we depended on to make our home. We could have roots in all those lands, and also flit between them all, and still feel at home. Home could be any and all of those places, and none of them. Home was inside me, in the essence of me I'd fought so hard to recover.

All of that was true, but at that moment in March, looking across the sofa at my husband, home was also completely where I was, physically, at that time.

Home could not be a flight away. Home could not be somewhere I was living out of a suitcase. Home could not be a place where we would have to go out looking for the things we would need.

So, for all my talk of wings-not-roots, of layers of home, the palimpsest of place, of purpose on the move and making a nest wherever we may be, in a crisis, the place mattered.

In the storm, the port mattered.

We didn't go back.

I think Michael's heart was in the same place as mine, even if his head needed convincing. He kept his eyes on flights for the next few days until the borders did indeed close. And as it turned out, for more than my indulgent emotional reasons, Denmark was one of the best places to be in 2020. Like everywhere else, schools and businesses closed in favour of working from home, and non-essential travel in and out of the country was banned. But it was not a hard lockdown as other countries experienced it. We were free to move around the country, with social distancing, and spend as much time as we liked walking in the neighbourhood. Perhaps because Denmark was the first European country after Italy to impose restrictions, the numbers of cases stayed low. By summer, everything had reopened, with social distancing and reduced capacity, and we enjoyed a summer tour of the country that felt almost normal. We weren't even wearing masks until late in 2020.

We didn't cross any borders for over a year. After a second lockdown period in early 2021, the country completely opened up again in the spring, leaving us with a short window to reconnect with our community there before we were due to leave Denmark that summer. The intensity of that time of rekindling and cementing friendships, of bringing projects to fruition, along with the fact of having been bound together within the confines of the house and the confines of a country, meant that in Denmark we were more deeply rooted than we had been anywhere else.

***

When I do go back, when I am living in one place, in a home we own, when the children have been going to the same school for five years or more, will I be uncomfortable in the certainty of it, in the certainty and solidity of my granite home in the granite city? Will I wish to be back in a liminal, in-between existence, surrounded by people who know and feel that transient space?

Years ago, navigating life in France, and then in Uganda, I used to have days where I would ache for normality. I would cave in with the cascade of new things and culture shock, at what I understand now to be a constant cycle of internal processing as we compare what we know from before to what we live now. As I caved in and the armour fell off, I would cry, I would scream, I would yell, 'I just want things to be NORMAL!' like a child who wants to go home, who is crying for their mother. I would ache for the familiar and the known; I would crave not having to interpret everything or translate everything, whether linguistically or culturally or geographically.

I don't have those days any more.

And when the crunch came, the crisis of a pandemic, when the need for comfort and security and familiarity was stronger than it had ever been? When what I would need most in navigating an uncertain, unfamiliar, ever-shifting set of circumstances, was exactly that sense of normal?

In a place between places, where I was foreign, in my nomadic tribe, in my third culture, in my temporary nest...I was already home.

EPILOGUE

It's spring 2023 as I write, and of course, a lot more has shifted in the last three years. We did leave Denmark in summer 2021, and it was the hardest goodbye I'd ever made. With lockdown over, I leaned in hard to our life there for the two months we had left, but so much felt undone, there was still potential bristling at every turn.

I'm writing now from Paris, where we've lived for nearly two years. This was another dream destination: the ultimate city experience, in a country where the language and culture were already completely familiar. The thrill of the city of lights has never worn off – you can see plenty of pictures at my Instagram @catrionaturnerbooks.

In our Parisian suburb home, despite all the hard-won lessons I've shared, I still struggle with that balance between temporary nesting and feeling fully settled. We have a bigger space to fill than we expected. The knowledge of 'just two years', as it's been from the start, has kept our furnishings to a minimum, and I've never felt fully at ease in the house. (Except in the bed. We still have the bed.) But in every other way, I've leaned into the possibilities here, with friendships, exploring, and creative projects, including exhilarating theatre performances.

And now, our two years are up.

What's next?

Well, the moment has come. We're moving to Aberdeen, after fourteen years away. It's all over.

Or is it?

Perhaps after such a long time, our original 'home' will feel like a new, unfamiliar, foreign location. It certainly will be for the boys, who have never lived there, although they have been asking for it for a long time. Will they find easy connection to their heritage? Or will they feel like hidden immigrants? Can I fit in to a life I once had, or will I need to create new community and opportunities? Have I changed too much to ever belong in just one place? What will the hardest challenges be, and what surprising joys will I discover?

They say repatriation is the hardest move. If you want to follow along and find out if that's true, you can! I'm writing the follow-up to *Nest* in real time, sharing a chapter each month with my Patreon supporters. Click the link for more details: https://www.patreon.com/CatrionaTurner

***

A heartfelt thank you for reading my story. If you enjoyed it, the most helpful thing you can do for me is leave a review on your favourite bookish platform. It helps new readers find the book. And let's stay connected! I'd love to know what resonated, what insights surprised you, or any questions you have about where we lived or what came next. Email me: catriona@thefrustratednester.com

***

If you want more to read right now, sign up for regular email updates and exclusive writing, and the first thing in your inbox will be the story of how Michael and I met, our meet-cute, the prologue to the whole adventure. Sign up here: https://thefrustratednester.com/read-more/

Acknowledgements

I nevitably, there are untold stories that I wanted to include, but fitting ten years into one book requires a process of selection. Here's a shout-out for the names that didn't make it into the pages: Brigita, Aziza, Srishti, Ekhlass, Alex, Birgit, David, Erin, Kaia, Scott, Amna, Bjorn, Stephanie, Marina, Ira, Carolyn, Cecile, Angie, Meg, Betina, Lucy, Magde, Mary, Bonnie – and Lindsey – thank you for the globe.

The rest of you will have to read the book to find yourself in its pages!

The book itself wouldn't be here without the support of people I'm lucky to know (and one I don't know).

Rachael Herron taught me everything about writing a memoir, and gave me limitless encouragement and ambition. I treasure her mentorship and her community.

Vig Gleeson went from accountability partner to friend, across Zoom, almost instantly. She has been by my side week by week, sharing the path to publication, and helping me get out my own way and connect to my instincts.

I'm grateful to Keri Bloomfield – thanks to her for doing it first and showing the way, for her support and encouragement, and for always being willing to get into the weeds with me. The invitation to join her Danish summerhouse writing retreat was the ultimate gift. Keri – may I always be your Dawn French in writing.

Lisa Webb has been a partner in creative projects between Pau and Pointe-Noire and beyond. I'm grateful for the ambition she fostered, and her trust in me as a bookish confidante.

Joanna Penn doesn't know me but has been a distance mentor with her podcast *The Creative Penn*; the knowledge she freely shares has instilled in me deep confidence for this process.

Thanks to my editing clients, who expand my writing community and let me immerse myself in sentences. It all feeds into a virtuous circle.

I have an inspiring creative community around me, including Usha, Dani, Noélie, Tara, and Lesli – our conversations and connections always spark something exciting.

Thanks to Paul Palmer-Edwards for the cover design that tuned into exactly what I wanted, and to Jessie Cunniffe for the blurb magic.

I'm grateful to my editor Rebecca Hendry, who brought the clarity and insight I knew this book needed when I'd spent three years in amongst it, too close to unravel the narrative. Thanks to Carol Wakeling for her eagle-eyed proofreading and insightful tidying-up.

Wayne Milstead at Circle of Missé gave me that first push of encouragement and showed me I was already a writer. With Aaron Tighe, they provided the perfect conditions for writing and creativity to flourish. I was deeply saddened when we lost Wayne earlier this year. This book is infused with his influence, and it benefitted from his insightful and gentle guidance when I returned to Missé in 2022.

Thanks to my mum and my brother for their patience and indulgence – for everything. My dad would have been beside himself with pride today. May this book and the other things we make and put into the world be part of his creative legacy.

Finally, thanks to Michael, Cameron, and Ben, for all they do to make me fully me. Yes, now I'm at home wherever they are.

About the Author

Catriona Turner is a Scottish writer and editor. Before living abroad, she worked as an English teacher in Scottish schools. She has since spent fourteen years globally mobile with her family, living in France (three times), Uganda, Congo, and Denmark.

Her first book, *Nest: a memoir of home on the move*, was published in June 2023, and she is now working on a follow-up memoir of returning to Scotland. Her writing has also appeared in anthologies, and she had a regular column in *The International* in Denmark.

Catriona has a passion for theatre and has been lucky enough to perform on stages in five countries. When she's not working with words or rehearsing, she relaxes with old movies and a needle and thread, or just hangs out with her boys while they make her laugh.

You can read more of Catriona's writing at catrionaturner.com. Find her proofreading and copyediting services at thewordbothy.com.

Made in the USA
Las Vegas, NV
06 June 2023

73059973R00152